# The Design of Literature

## THE PENDULUM LITERATURE SERIES

■ The Design of Literature

☐ The Design of Drama

☐ The Design of the Narrative

☐ The Design of Poetry

# The Design of Literature

LAWRENCE BUELL

JEANNE BAY, *EDITORIAL CONSULTANT*
*CHAIRMAN, ENGLISH DEPARTMENT*
*OBERLIN HIGH SCHOOL*

Pendulum Press, Inc.
West Haven, Connecticut

*FOR KIM*

˟

*ISBN   0-88301-077-1 Complete Set*
     *0-88301-078-X This Volume*

*Library of Congress Catalog Card Number 73-75452*

*Published by*
Pendulum Press, Inc.
The Academic Building
Saw Mill Road
West Haven, Connecticut  06516

Printed in the United States of America

Cover Design by Dick Brassil, Silverman Design Group

Typography by Selectype

# CONTENTS

Literature, Good Literature,
and Ordinary Writing   9   *Chapter One*

Four Basic Approaches to Literature   23   *Chapter Two*

The Analytical Approach: A Closer Look   35   *Chapter Three*

The Four Critical Approaches in Action   60   *Chapter Four*

Reading Literature From Different Periods   74   *Chapter Five*

Writing About Literature   91   *Chapter Six*

Appendix   104

Bibliography   109

## ABOUT THE AUTHOR

Lawrence Buell received a B.A. from Princeton University, and an M.A. and Ph.D. from Cornell University. He has taught at Tunghai University in Taiwan and is Associate Professor of English and Dean of Admissions at Oberlin College.

Mr. Buell is a Woodrow Wilson Fellow and a Princeton-in-Asia Fellow. He has published articles on American literature in *American Quarterly, American Literature,* and other scholarly journals. Cornell University Press is soon to publish his book *Transcendentalism: Style and Vision in the American Renaissance.*

## PREFACE

*The Design of Literature* is one in a series of four related but independent texts. The other three volumes deal in detail with the narrative, drama, and poetry. This study discusses the problems of understanding and writing about literature in general. Although it is designed for students who have recently begun to study literature in depth, the questions it raises are universal for all readers. What is good literature? What should I look for when I read? What can I say about this particular book? What makes it succeed or fail as a literary work? However long they study literature, thoughtful readers continue to ask questions like these. With experience, their answers become more perceptive. But as long as they enjoy reading, they continue to return to these perennial issues.

I have tried throughout to write in clear, layman's language, yet at the same time not to oversimplify the complexity of literature. I have assumed from the outset that the study of literature is an inexact science, the goal of which is to be as specific about its subject as possible but no more, so that justice is done both to what can and what cannot be proven about it. I have tried also to convey the sense of enjoyment felt by those who teach and write about literature for a living. Perhaps the most essential purpose of this book, in fact, is to demonstrate that literary analysis need not be a solemn, joyless activity, engaged in merely to satisfy a requirement. Once its methods become familiar, it can also be a great deal of fun.

# ACKNOWLEDGMENTS

Grateful acknowledgment is made to the authors and publishers who granted permission to reprint the following selections:

James Joyce. *Ulysses.* Excerpt reprinted by permission of The Bodley Head Ltd. and Random House Inc.

Wallace Stevens. "Anecdote of the Jar." Copyright 1923, renewed 1951 by Wallace Stevens. From *The Collected Poems of Wallace Stevens.* Reprinted by permission of Alfred A. Knopf Inc. and Faber and Faber Ltd.

William Butler Yeats. "Long-Legged Fly." Copyright 1940 by Georgie Yeats, renewed 1968 by Bertha Georgie Yeats, Michael Butler Yeats, and Anne Yeats. Excerpt reprinted by permission of Michael Butler Yeats, Macmillan & Co. Ltd., Macmillan Co. of Canada Ltd., and the Macmillan Company.

# CHAPTER ONE

# LITERATURE, GOOD LITERATURE, AND ORDINARY WRITING

**DEFINING LITERATURE**

The word *literature* can be used in several ways, which to some extent contradict each other. To prepare for what comes later, it may help to point out these differences now.

Usually *literature* calls to mind a certain group of writings which are somehow particularly creative or artistic, whose quality makes them superior to the ordinary run of printed matter. The novels of Charles Dickens or Fyodor Dostoyevsky, for example, are considered to be literature; the novels of Mickey Spillane are not. They are classified instead as popular fiction. The Nancy Drew or Hardy Boys stories might be called children's literature, but not elevated to the same level as the works of James Joyce or William ·Faulkner. Newspapers, for the most part, are not considered literature, but the essays of some talented journalists, like George Orwell and Ernest Hemingway, are thought to qualify.

On the other hand, any poem, story, or play tends to be considered as more literary than journalism and other nonfictional prose, regardless of artistic quality. It seems more natural to think of any best-selling novel as literature than the writings of Sir Winston Churchill, even though Churchill was a better writer than most professional novelists. The reason for this is, of course, that the novel is a more purely imaginative or creative form of writing than nonfiction.

In still another of its meanings, however, *literature* is used much more broadly to refer to anything whatsoever which has been written about a given subject, as when a tourist asks a travel agent for his literature about Europe. This is in fact the original meaning of the word. Historically speaking, *literature* was derived from the Latin word for "letters" of the alphabet and was used, until the nineteenth century, to mean simply "writing." Magazines, scientific works, philosophical treatises were all once included under the heading of literature and indeed still are in some histories of literature written by scholars today.

Finally, to add one further complication, it is often argued that the definition of literature should include not only the written word but the spoken word as well. Surely folk songs, oral narratives, and orations are also literary works, in the sense that they are created out of words, even if they are never actually recorded on paper.

Altogether then, *literature* can be defined in three main ways: (1) as an inclusive term, to mean anything made out of words; (2) to refer to good writing (or oral composition) as opposed to mediocre; (3) to apply to works of imagination as opposed to nonfiction. These three meanings blend together in actual usage.

Literature courses and books about literary appreciation are mostly concerned with literature in the second and third senses. Their main purposes are to give you an understanding of what "good" writing is, so that you will want to read more of it and perhaps even produce it on your own, and to introduce you to the kinds of literature which are most original and imaginative. Therefore, most of what this book says about literature refers to works of high artistic quality and especially to poetry, drama, and narrative; each of these three literary forms is discussed in depth in another volume in this series. Do not conclude from this, however, that other forms of literary expression are not literature or that writing which does not have great artistic value has no place in literary study. On the contrary, it would be truer to say that almost any piece of writing is in some sense a product of the imagination and must be appreciated as such if it is to be fully understood. *The Autobiography of Benjamin Franklin,* for instance, reads like a fictional success story, because the author has chosen to represent those details which fit his vision of his career as a fulfillment of what we now call the American dream. Indeed, any record of an eventful life is apt to resemble a novel, presenting a steady development of character, plot, and theme through a series of episodes.

Literary art expression is also an important aspect of many works of history, philosophy, religion, and social science, not only in the sense that many authors in these fields write good prose, but also in the sense that their ideas themselves must often be interpreted somewhat poetically, as creative suggestions rather than as statements of actual facts. For example, Sigmund Freud, the father of modern clinical psychology, compared the reconstruction of a patient's case history with the writing of fiction. Some historians have gone so far as to define history itself as a form of fiction, a retelling of a series of events from the author's point of view. Studies of slavery in America, for example, would certainly fit this definition, as they have inevitably reflected the values of the author and the period in which they were written. Even the most objective historical studies have proved to be a mixture of fact and myth.

Rather than identify literature, then, with stories or poems or any other particular form of writing, it may be better to think of it more broadly as the element of fiction or creative expression in all writing. The line between the philosophy of Albert Camus, who liked to present his ideas in narrative form, and the tales of Nathaniel Hawthorne, a writer who was obsessed with moral ideas, is impossible to draw. Many of the same features you will be taught to look for when reading novels can be found in your local newspaper, which also tells stories, develops characters, and uses language for the sake of effect. To realize this—that the magazine you are reading is partly a piece of fiction—may make you more continuously aware of the various ways in which language can be used creatively; and it may also, in some cases, protect you against taking what you read too quickly at face value. Consider, for example, the following reports of the same imaginary political appearance:

1. Attention was called to the extraordinary amounts of taxpayer money spent by Congressman Dribble on travel between his home and Washington. Dribble denied any wrongdoing, insisting that he simply wanted to "keep in touch with the folks back home."

2. One member of the audience questioned whether Congressman Dribble had spent too much on travel between Washington and his home. The congressman explained the situation by noting that any responsible legislator must "keep in touch with the folks back home."

In these two passages, the *facts* reported are about the same, but the overall effects are opposite. The first passage puts Dribble in the worst possible light; the second strongly defends him. Altogether, whatever actually happened has been transformed in each case by the imagination of the reporter, and the finished products are at least as much works of fiction as records of fact.

It would be wrong to insist upon calling these two imaginary newspaper accounts literature, since they neither succeed in being very creative nor were they intended to be. They are included here only to illustrate the fact that writings which most people suppose are non-literary actually do contain some of the same fictive qualities as poetry, narrative, and drama. After you have become familiar with the methods of literary study described later in this book, you may find it interesting—and instructive—to try applying them to writing which is usually considered non-literary. For the present, however, we need to concentrate on learning how to understand and evaluate works of literature in the sense of good writing or oral composition.

## JUDGING WHAT IS GOOD LITERATURE

The high school student is occasionally required to read a book which his English teacher likes but he doesn't. The last time this happened to you, perhaps you remained silent but wondered how the teacher could be so out of touch. Or perhaps you asked, "Why did you want us to read *that?*" If so, the reply may not have been satisfactory, because the question is far too complicated to answer in a few words—as you yourself know if you have ever been called upon to defend a literary preference of your own which someone else considered ridiculous.

The question, however, is worth trying to answer. The essential reason for talking about a book in the first place is to understand and communicate what impressed you as good or bad about it. The rest of this chapter, therefore, will attempt to pinpoint several basic factors which influence one's judgment as to whether or not a piece of literature is good.

□ *Personal Preference vs. Personal Growth.* To begin with, you should realize that your notion of what is good literature is constantly changing. Your literary likes and dislikes will continue to develop as long as your mind does. At age five, you probably thought that *The Tale of Peter Rabbit* was good. Although you may still enjoy reading it to your little brother, the chances are that it is no longer your favorite book. Likewise, a teacher's first response when the class doesn't like the assignment may be "Oh, they aren't ready for it yet." The poet-critic T.S. Eliot once remarked, for example, that it takes a lifetime to understand Dante's *The Divine Comedy.* William Faulkner claimed that he reread Miguel de Cervantes' novel *Don Quixote* every year and made new discoveries with each reading. Indeed there may be some works which only an aged person can fully understand, like Shakespeare's tragedy of *King Lear,* the hero of which is an old king betrayed by his ungrateful daughters and his own short-sightedness.

In other words, one cannot expect to appreciate some literature, including a number of works which are often called great, until he has reached a certain stage of life or educational development. Before then, it may sometimes seem almost as if they had been written in a foreign language. One's first reaction to Shakespeare is often boredom, and it is not until after having read more of his works and having seen several performances that one's attitude is likely to change. This is probably a stage almost everyone must go through before being able to appreciate the literature of four hundred years ago.

Of course, no matter how educated you become, your tastes may never agree fully with those of your instructors. Nor should they, necessarily. For example, one of the literary works most frequently taught in American high school English courses is George Eliot's *Silas Marner,* and yet experts disagree sharply as to whether or not it is a really "good" novel. Each reader has his own particular range of sensitivity, which will inevitably cause him to overvalue some kinds of writing and undervalue others. Or to put this idea in a more positive light, he will have a special feeling for the fine points of some writers and a gift for exposing the faults of others. For this reason, any thoughtful teacher will welcome intelligent disagreement over the merits of a book, even from students who are much less experienced readers than he. Through this process, the teacher develops his own private list of writers and works to which he knows he responds eccentrically, for better or worse. By the same token, students should become self-critical to the point that they are aware of their own strengths and limitations as readers.

☐ *The Tastes of the Age vs. Enduring Values.* A person's reaction to literature depends not only upon his level of personal development, but also upon the age and environment in which he lives. A young man from Watts and a debutante from Virginia are apt to react very differently to *Gone With the Wind* and *The Autobiography of Malcolm X.* In the nineteenth century, Henry Wadsworth Longfellow was acclaimed as America's greatest poet; today he is virtually unread, except for a very few poems. Longfellow's contemporary Walt Whitman, on the other hand, was largely ignored in his own day but is now regarded as the father of modern American poetry.

As a way of resolving such differences and shifts of opinion, it is often said that one can tell whether a book is good if it has stood the test of time. Appeal to discerning readers over a long period of history is taken as evidence that the book is excellent, and it is called a *classic.* You should not allow yourself automatically to be impressed with this line of argument, because (a) it does you little good to know a book is a classic unless you can see it for yourself, and (b) classics are always in the process of being revalued, like any literary work. Virgil's epic the *Aeneid*, for instance, was once considered superior to Homer's *Iliad* and *Odyssey* on the ground that Virgil preserved and refined Homer's best points while avoiding his mistakes. Today, however, Homer is considered superior, partly because he is more original. Still, no educated person has disputed the fact that both works are classics, and for centuries both were required reading for students in Europe and America. Knowing this should at least give you a basic respect for Homer and Virgil and make you inclined to doubt yourself rather than them if they put you to sleep the first time through. You may never feel really at home with them, but the attempt will have been worthwhile if it gives you a better understanding about what it is in yourself and them which makes such a rapport impossible.

□ *Popular vs. Serious Literature.* Perhaps the most important reason for differences in individual literary judgment is that there are two different levels on which literature is written and read. The same reader will tend to approach a "great" novel like Dostoyevsky's *Crime and Punishment* in a very different frame of mind from the way in which he reads the latest best-seller. He expects to be more entertained by the latter, to be quickly swept up in the plot and transported to whatever imaginary world is being described. He also expects to be fascinated by Dostoyevsky, but in another way. He realizes that *Crime and Punishment* is going to be much more difficult to understand, and that it will not simply excite him but also challenge his mind and increase his awareness of the nature of justice and how the human mind works under stress. The first reading will very likely be more intense but also more superficial. The second will probably have a more lasting impact.

To a certain extent, we can distinguish between authors on the same basis, between those whose primary motive is to achieve a commercial success by providing entertainment for a mass audience, and those whose ultimate goal is to create literature which is original and excellent regardless of its commercial appeal. The first type of writer generally is called *popular,* and the second *serious.* This distinction is not hard and fast. Many authors have written on both levels at once (like Dickens and Hemingway); some have set out to write popular literature and wound up becoming serious writers (like Herman Melville); and some books and writers are so close to the borderline between the two categories that it is impossible to fit them into one or the other. Carl Sandburg, Somerset Maugham, John Hersey, and Kurt Vonnegut Jr. are all examples of this sort. It is quite possible, then, for serious literature to have a popular appeal, and it is also quite possible to read popular literature in a serious way. Extensive studies, for instance, have been written on the content and publication of comic books and detective stories, using some of the methods which will be described in the next two chapters. Still, it is fair to draw a general distinction between writers and works whose basic purpose is to entertain you and those whose purpose is to express a personal vision of life and make a lasting contribution to literary history.

*Popular* and *serious* are somewhat loaded terms which imply a bias against the first and in favor of the second. In fact, it is impossible to say categorically that one is superior to the other, because they appeal to somewhat different sides of a reader's personality. There are times, for instance, when anybody prefers—and needs—to escape into the world of the wild west, situation comedy, or science fiction and at such times he should not be forced to read Homer instead. Any intelligent person who reads *only* popular literature, however, is limiting his range of experience considerably. The case for reading serious literature is that it can engage your whole mind and not just a superficial part. If you persist at it, you will expand your mind beyond what you thought possible. It will make you more aware of all the ways in which language can be used for beauty and effect; it will make you a wiser judge of character and of the relationships between people; it will give you a better understanding of the relationship between ideas and reality, of the way ideals do or do not work out in practice; it will make you more aware of how other minds work and of the conditions of life in other times and places. In short, it will make you a more intelligent and humane person—unless, of course, you become preoccupied with literature at the expense of living and do nothing except read books. But that is not a real danger for most people, even teachers of literature.

As an example of the differences in the experience of reading popular and serious literature, let us look at a group of works which appeal in one way or other to a very common impulse: the desire to transcend one's ordinary, human limitations and do some heroic action. On the most popular level, in comic strip situations this transformation is simply taken for granted. The skinny boy on the beach has sand kicked in his face, goes home and exercises, and in the next scene has turned into a mountain of muscle who easily knocks out the bully and wins the girl. The moral of the story is, of course, "You can do it too." The adventures of Superman work in the same way. When disaster strikes, mild-mannered Clark Kent instantly becomes the all-powerful savior of the city. The reader does not picture himself as the hero in the same way as in the muscle-building ad, but in each case the story appeals to the same simple, secret, widespread wish that ordinary people are really supermen in disguise. And in each case the results are quick, exciting and decisive; the wish is easily satisfied—perhaps too easily, so that afterwards we feel a little amused or disgusted with ourselves for having been taken in.

The James Bond stories of Ian Fleming are slightly more plausible versions of the Superman theme. But here too, for the most part, the hero is designed to satisfy the simple desire to see—or to be—an all-powerful figure who can be counted on to be the absolute master of almost any situation. Here too, the real pleasure of reading is that it provides an escape into a world where the impossible can happen, where life is always exciting, and where one's practical problems are left behind.

Most serious literature also provides a kind of escape, but not a complete one. Serious literature might be said to begin at the point when the author makes it impossible for the reader to forget entirely about reality. The reader is made conscious of a conflict between the actual world and the world of imagination, when the imaginary world begins to be pictured as having real and insoluble problems of its own.

A good example of a story which is on the borderline between popular and serious literature is James Thurber's "The Secret Life of Walter Mitty." Most of the "action" consists of Mitty's daydreams of grandeur as he accompanies his wife on a trip to the hairdresser's. In quick succession, Mitty pictures himself as a hero in battle, a millionaire, and an eminent surgeon. But the reader is not swept up by these fantasies in the way he would be if he were reading a James Bond story. On the contrary, Thurber's purpose is to induce the reader to laugh at his own romantic impulses by contrasting the fantasies of an ordinary person like himself with the humdrum, everyday, shopping trip situation.

Thurber does not develop the secret life of Walter Mitty very far, however. The story hinges on a simple contrast between dream and reality; nothing is revealed about Mitty except that he is a dreamer; we do not know whether he is happy or unhappy, what his marriage is like, or whether his childhood was traumatic. Though Thurber's story pokes fun at people's escapist impulses, in another sense it reinforces them. We see Mitty as a silly but essentially lovable character: he enjoys his dream world; his imagination causes no harm. In the long run, reading about him may even encourage us in our own daydreaming by reinforcing our suspicion that everybody else is doing the same thing. After reading Thurber we may feel a little more self-conscious and sheepish about our fantasies of greatness but also more inclined to indulge in them as an enjoyable and socially accepted pleasure.

A more serious-minded writer might look at Walter Mitty's situation somewhat differently. He might see Mitty as a pathetic figure, unable to cope with the real world, and regard his daydreams as an effort to compensate for some previous failure or disappointment. A case in point is Arthur Miller's play, *Death of a Salesman*. The main character, Willy Loman, is obsessed with another vision of instant greatness. For him it is the American dream of success. The play shows how Willy is tragically unable to realize this dream and how he ruins his life and virtually destroys his family in the process of trying. Much more than Walter Mitty, Willy appears to be a complete human being who inspires a mixture of sympathy and disapproval, and whose story is designed both to appeal to the side of the reader which is like Willy and to make him reflect upon the consequences of becoming too engrossed in one's own visions of success.

To qualify as serious literature, however, a work does not have to be tragic. Take, for instance, still another example of the theme we have been tracing, James Joyce's novel *Ulysses*. Joyce's main character, Leopold Bloom, is also a somewhat unhappy middle-aged man, living on the edge of poverty and distracted to a large extent by the memory of past hopes and disappointments. But Joyce puts his career in a different light from Willy's by comparing Bloom (as Bloom compares himself) to other, more famous drifters of history and legend, like Ulysses and the Wandering Jew. The result is a mixture of the comic, the pathetic, the heroic, and the purely bizarre. For example, Bloom's rather disconnected activities during the one day in which the novel takes place are likened to the twenty-year wanderings of Ulysses. When Bloom happens to get the better of the ex-shot put champion of Ireland during a barroom argument, he is comically compared to Ulysses defeating the giant cyclops Polyphemus. Through such means, Bloom comes across, on the one hand, as just an ordinary urban type, while on the other hand, he is both dignified and made to look ridiculous by being described as an epic hero. And the reader of *Ulysses* is left with similarly mixed feelings about the significance of his own daily dreams and wanderings.

Our list of examples could be extended indefinitely, but perhaps enough has been said to let us draw some conclusions. (a) The difference between serious literature and popular literature has less to do with subject matter than with its treatment. Love can be the subject of the tritest poems as well as the greatest. Superman comics illustrate the dream of greatness just as markedly as *Death of a Salesman* and may, therefore, be equally if not more interesting as an object of study to a historian of American culture. The difference is that Miller's play treats the theme in a more subtle way and does much more justice to its complexities. (b) In general, serious writers try to explore or at least suggest as many of the possibilities of their subjects as they can, while popular literature tends to reduce its subjects to variations on familiar formulas. (c) Serious literature is not necessarily tragic or even solemn. The best comic writers have always been just as serious about their work as the best tragedians.

Don't be under any illusions that the preceding discussion has fully prepared you to determine whether a given work is serious literature and, if so, just how good it is. As noted above, some works are extremely difficult to pigeonhole, and in any case literary judgments differ from era to era, from individual to individual, and within the lifetime of the same individual. In the next chapter, we shall take a closer look at the reasons for these differences in judgment.

# CHAPTER TWO

# FOUR BASIC APPROACHES TO LITERATURE

### THE FOUR APPROACHES DESCRIBED

The problem of learning to appreciate what is good in literature is complicated by the fact that the same work can be viewed in four different ways. It can be read (1) as a representation or imitation of real life; (2) as an expression of the life and values of the author; (3) as a way of influencing or appealing to an audience; and (4) as a stylistic achievement, constructed according to various literary techniques and existing in and for itself independently of its relation to author, audience, and the reality it represents. These four approaches are sometimes called: (1) *mimetic*, (2) *expressive*, (3) *pragmatic*, (4) *objective* or *analytical.* *

The *mimetic* approach is the oldest of the four

---

*The first and last of these terms are very widely used. The other three are heard less often, but they have been popularized to some extent from having been used in M.H. Abrams' influential study of literary history, *The Mirror and the Lamp: Romantic Theory and The Critical Tradition.* Chapter One of that book outlines the four approaches, and the history of their uses. Abrams' discussion is too detailed and technical for the introductory student, but those who want to learn more about the subject after mastering the contents of this chapter will find it a very useful essay.

approaches to literature. It predominated during the classical era and formed the basis for the criticism of the first great literary critics* in Western history, Plato and Aristotle.

The mimetic critic looks at literature, so to speak, as a mirror of life, and he tends to value literary works according to the faithfulness with which they portray society and human nature. Hamlet, for instance, was speaking as a mimetic critic when he urged the troupe of wandering actors "to hold, as 'twere, the mirror up to nature." Notice, however, that Hamlet is not demanding that a play be "realistic" in the literal sense of creating the illusion of everyday life, like a documentary film or a movie set which looks exactly like the interior of a contemporary living room. This is only one kind of imitation. An artist may choose to ignore or defy this kind of realism in order to do a more effective job of representing inner emotions, such as when Shakespeare uses the "unrealistic" technique of soliloquy in order to convey a much fuller sense of what Hamlet is thinking than would otherwise be possible.

The thoughtful mimetic critic, then, does not insist that a work be literally true, or that it deal with everyday reality. He recognizes caricature, romance, epic poetry, and other non-realistic forms of literature as legitimate ways of representing reality. In approaching these and other types of works, his main question is not "How realistic is this work?" so much as "In what sense is it realistic?" or "What kind of reality does it represent?" "How does the work reflect the society and values of its

---

*A *critic* is a person who studies and perhaps writes about literature in a serious way, like Abrams. His book is a work of *criticism*, as is any written discussion of literature. Discussions of individual literary works are sometimes called *practical* or *applied* criticism, in contrast to *critical theory*, or discussion of general approaches to literature.

day?" or "How does it portray the reality which it is supposed to represent?"

Two important kinds of modern mimetic criticism are: (1) studies of literature as a reflection of social customs and ideology and (2) studies of the concept of reality in various writers and works. Good examples of the first kind include the writings of the Marxist critic Georg Lukacs and the American Lionel Trilling; a distinguished example of the second is Eric Auerbach, *Mimesis: the Representation of Reality in Western Literature*. At this stage, you may find these and some of the other critical writings suggested too difficult for you, but you should be aware of them as significant critical works. For the present, the bibliography at the back of this book will suggest some additional readings which are designed to explain the mimetic and other major critical approaches especially for high school and college students in somewhat more detail than the present chapter.

The *pragmatic* approach focuses on the relation between the work and its audience. This relation can be seen in one or both of two main ways, depending upon the nature of the work and the taste of the reader. The work can be viewed *didactically,* as a means of setting forth a philosophy or code of values, or it can be viewed *affectively,* as an emotional stimulus having a given effect on the reader's feelings.

The first of these two approaches has been very popular ever since pragmatic criticism came into its own during the Middle Ages. Today the question students most commonly ask about a book is still "What is its philosophy of life?"— which is the basic issue in didactic interpretation as a whole. Indeed the majority of thoughtful readers probably are didactic critics in the sense that they value literature which "has something to say." However, the meaning or the philosophical element of a work is much more important in some cases than others. A situation comedy, for instance, will naturally have much less to do with philosophy than a religious narrative like *Pilgrim's Progress,* where the author's avowed purpose is to dramatize the journey of the human soul from sinfulness to salvation. And even a book of the latter sort is more than just a manual of instruction. It does not simply outline a set of doctrines; it presents them in fictional form.

This distinction is easy to forget; and over the years didactic criticism has too often tried to make literature into something it is not, either by reducing it to absolute moral statements, or by insisting that artists should observe or even advocate a particular system of values in their work. Those who take such positions are often more interested in upholding the social order than in understanding literature itself. For this reason the term "didactic" has come to be associated in recent years with narrow-mindedness and intolerance; and most present-day readers who like to approach literature as a means of conveying ideas prefer not to call themselves didactic critics. For although they do tend to be especially interested in literary works which deal with philosophical and moral questions in a serious way, they do not insist that literature express a definite moral position. They ask not simply "What is the author's philosophy of life?" but also: "How seriously are the ideas in this work to be taken? How important are they to the work as a whole? Is the work meant primarily as a dramatization or expression of a particular set of values, or is the author merely playing with the ideas he uses?" and "What are the various ways in which the author conveys a point of view or standard of judgment in the work?"

A fine example of a critical work which deals with this last question is Wayne Booth, *The Rhetoric of Fiction.*

Two other important modern critics whose work has much to say about the relationship between literature and ideas or values are Yvor Winters and C.S. Lewis.

Affective criticism devotes most of its attention to the audience's reaction to a work, rather than to the message or content of the work itself. On the most elementary level this kind of criticism consists merely of reporting one's likes and dislikes about a work. Beyond this, however, the affective critic will ask "Why does this work move me as it does? Is my reaction typical or eccentric? What kind of emotional effect, in general, does literature have on people? Why do people read literature at all?" Increasing attention has been paid to these deceptively simple questions during the past fifty years, as a result of the rise of interest in psychology.

Generally speaking, there are two kinds of affective criticism: that which relies on common sense reactions and judgments, and that which makes use of the discoveries of modern clinical psychology. An interesting example of the first is I.A. Richards, *Practical Criticism,* which analyzes the reactions of a group of people to a series of poems which Richards asked them to evaluate. An example of the second is Simon O. Lesser, *Fiction and the Unconscious,* which explains the imaginative appeal of literature in psychoanalytical terms.

*Expressive* criticism looks at literature as an extension of the personality of the writer. This approach is more recent than the first two. It emerged around 1800 as part of the Romantic movement, which celebrated the importance of individual self-expression and originality, in contrast to the so-called classical principles of proportion and adherence to generally accepted standards of taste. A typical statement of romantic expressivism is the poet Walt Whitman's exclamation:

> . . .this is no book,
> Who touches this touches a man, . . .
> I spring from the pages into your arms.

Few readers today would accept the more extreme notions of Whitman and some of his contemporaries, such as the idea that a literary work should be judged by its *sincerity,* or the faithfulness with which it exhibits the deepest needs and desires of its author. (For one thing, it is clear that no amount of earnestness can produce a good poem if the author doesn't know how to write.) Still, most would probably agree that sincerity in the sense of commitment to one's work is indispensible to the creation of great art. And most readers would also agree that *originality* is an important quality in literature. To this extent, we too can be said to live in a "post-romantic" age.

Like Whitman, the modern expressivist reader will naturally take a special interest in literature which is strongly autobiographical, and tend to value that which is most sensitively introspective and self-aware. But rather than stop with simple questions, "Is the work sincere? Is the artist a true man? ", he will go on to study the extent to which a literary work reproduces or distorts actual episodes in the life of the author, the degree to which this seems to be done consciously vs. unconsciously, and the ways in which the author's personality and background may have stimulated or inhibited him as an artist. In his investigations he will frequently make use of concepts from clinical psychology.

The most common type of modern criticism along expressive lines is the study which interprets the work of a particular author in terms of his life. One excellent example of this sort is the first volume of Roger Asselineau's two-part study, *The Evolution of Walt Whitman,* which might be consulted in connection with Chapter Four of this book.

A more readable although somewhat overingenious work is Philip Young's *Hemingway Reconsidered*, which traces the supposed impact of Hemingway's experiences in World War I upon the later development of his career as a writer.

*Objective* or *analytical* criticism looks at a work of literature as a coherent and intricate structure or organism. The main questions the analytical critic asks are: How is this work put together? How is it organized and unified, if at all? What are the principal recurring elements or patterns which control its development? What are the characteristic stylistic techniques used by the author? What is the relationship between the form and the content of the work? In pursuing these and related questions the analytical critic uses a battery of concepts and terms, the most important of which are described in the next chapter. Some of the qualities which he is apt to look for and prize most highly in literature are *ambiguity,* or richness of meaning and implication; *tension* and *paradox,* or the balancing of opposites against each other; and *economy,* or conciseness and care in the use of language and the organization of the work. The analytical critic regards such features as important for two main reasons. First, the value of literature for him consists largely in its craftsmanship, and the qualities in question require great technical sophistication on the writer's part. By the same token, these qualities generally point to a deeper and more complex awareness of life than is conveyed in literature which lacks them.

Sometimes this bias leads the critic into bad judgments: he is apt to overvalue works which are shallow but elaborately clever and to undervalue what is simple but profound. In concentrating on the structure of the work itself, furthermore, he runs the risk of ignoring the social, moral, and personal aspects of literature and thereby reducing literature to a mechanical contrivance. But the analytical approach can do a far better job than the other three of describing the actual tools of the literary trade and how they are used in the process of writing.

The analytical approach is by far the youngest of the four, having come into its own only during the past forty years or so. It is now, however, the prevailing type of criticism, and all students of literature now learn it and regularly make use of its techniques, even when their immediate purpose in writing is not analytical. Indeed, most knowledgeable readers today would agree that the analytical approach is more crucial than the other three, in the sense that it concentrates most closely upon the literary work itself and therefore reveals the most about the art of literature, whereas the other approaches deal with the connection between literature and history, biography, psychology, and other related subjects. Some of the first analytical critics even went so far as to argue that the other approaches are illegitimate, that all literature should be read entirely without reference to the times in which it was written, the life and intentions of the author, and its impact upon the reader. In retrospect it is clear that this position is non-sensical, but most readers continue to agree that an understanding of how a work is put together should be the first, if not the last job of the serious reader. The original advocates of the analytical approach are still called the *new critics* and the analytical approach as a whole is still sometimes described as *new critical*.

Perhaps the two commonest types of analytical criticism are: (1) explications or detailed analyses of particular literary works or a particular author's work as a whole; and (2) discussions of traditional literary genres, or forms (e.g., tragedy, comedy, epic poetry, the novel), and conventions. The second type differs from the first in tracing the same feature through a range of works, sometimes written centuries apart, rather than concentrating on a single work or writer. Some excellent, although difficult, examples of the first kind are included in Cleanth Brooks's collection of essays, *The Well Wrought Urn;* a very readable example of the second is E.M. Forster's *Aspects of the Novel.*

## THE APPROACHES COMPARED

Obviously four readers who were each disciples of one of the four approaches just discussed would have very different reactions to the same literary work. Let us say that they each read Ernest Hemingway's recollections of life among Paris literary circles during the 1920s, the so-called "Lost Generation" period, *A Moveable Feast.* This is a series of sketches in which all the leading writers of the day appear. Most of them are described rather sarcastically, to the point that the book almost seems to become an exercise in oneupsmanship, a way for Hemingway to settle his old grudges.

Since the book is one of Hemingway's's most autobiographical writings, it would be received with great interest by the expressivist. He would perhaps be disappointed that Hemingway does not reveal as much of himself as most writers do in their reminiscences; nevertheless, he would find the memoirs an important clue to Hemingway's personality, and he would be fascinated by the resemblances between the sketches in it and Hemingway's story-telling style. The mimetic critic would also be interested in *A Moveable Feast,* but primarily as a reflection of the life and values of the 1920s; and he might judge the book more harshly because of Hemingway's biased and self-serving portrayal of his fellow-writers and his relationship to them. Whereas the pragmatic reader would be intrigued by the fact that Hemingway as portrayed in his own memoirs acts very much like a Hemingway hero, the mimetic reader might take this as a sign of Hemingway's unconscious failure to distinguish reality from private fantasy. The pragmatic reader might examine Hemingway's memoirs as an embodiment of the familiar Hemingway code of values, which emphasizes masculinity, stoicism, bluntness, courage, and male companionship, as opposed to the "softer" virtues of tenderness, refinement, and the like. He would be sure to notice Hemingway's tendency to view his fellow-writers as sissies, phonies, and decadents by contrast to his own shrewd, rugged, engagingly boyish yet resolutely independent self. Or if the pragmatic reader was an affective critic, he might try to study the various ways in which *A Moveable Feast* appeals to these values and prejudices in the reader. In either case he would quickly conclude that it is crude stuff by comparison to Hemingway's best fiction. So would the objective or analytic reader, who would find that in its style and organization the book is by and large little more than an inferior version of Hemingway's short stories.

Of course these readers' interests are so different that all four would rarely want to read the same book in the first place. The mimetic reader might have a special preference for novels which deal with social issues; the pragmatic reader would tend to prefer the more philosophical writers, like Camus or Dostoyevsky; the expressive reader would prefer writers whose works reveal their own spiritual development, like William Wordsworth and D.H. Lawrence; the analytic reader would prefer the great literary craftsman, like Henry James and James Joyce. What kind of reader you are will depend on what kind of person you are. A social scientist, a clinical psychologist, a minister, an artist will almost inevitably have different literary likes and dislikes.

During the history of Western literature, furthermore, the four approaches have each been more or less in fashion at different points in time, as we have seen. The reasons for these various shifts in attitudes toward literature are much too complicated to explain in a brief study like this one, because they are entwined with larger and more far-reaching shifts in philosophical outlook. The present-day emphasis on analytical criticism, for example, is partly a manifestation of the scientific approach to problem-solving which has gradually taken over our way of thinking on many types of issues during the last hundred years. I have mentioned these changes in the history of attitudes towards literature simply as one more indication of how difficult it is to say flatly: "This work is better than that one." What we really mean by such a remark is "Assuming that x, y, and z are literary values, this work is superior." If you choose to take the position "What's good is what turns me on"—an extreme version of the affective approach—then you cannot be faulted on logical grounds for rating Donald Duck higher than *Hamlet,* although you might be faulted for intellectual underdevelopment.

Actually most readers use a combination of all the major critical approaches, including the critics mentioned above. No one is a purely mimetic or expressive critic. For the sake of convenience I have used these labels, but the fact is that the approaches blend with each other, and the differences between individual readers are usually ones of degree rather than of kind. Even the examples given above for each type of criticism actually make use of a combination of approaches.

All this is probably as true for you yourself as it is for the professional critic. Though you may not be conscious that you are following any kind of critical method, very likely you have indeed wondered about mimetic, pragmatic, expressive, and analytic questions in the course of reading through a book which interested you. "Is that really true?" "What's the point of this?" "I wonder what kind of person the author was." "Why does the book end that way?" All of these are questions which are important both to professional literary critics and to readers who have never "studied" literature at all and never read anything more challenging than the *Reader's Digest.*

Genuine literary appreciation begins when one becomes aware of his own interest in such questions and decides that he wants to find out more about them and other questions like them. No one can predict when and if this will happen to a person. Perhaps you have already had such an experience; if not, no teacher or guidebook like this can create it for you; you have to feel it yourself. But advice from others can help, by introducing you to books which you might find stimulating and by making you aware of some of the interesting and important questions you might raise about those books to make your reading of them more enjoyable and rewarding.

This chapter is designed as a first step toward the latter. The next chapter will give a much more detailed description of the analytical approach, which is the most crucial to the understanding of how literature is written and organized. After that, we shall see how all the major approaches can be applied in the case of a particular literary work.

# THE ANALYTICAL APPROACH: A CLOSER LOOK

## ANALYSIS AS A GAME OF THE MIND

Many inexperienced readers of literature find analysis a difficult and even painful chore. Students often say: "I don't like to analyze something I've enjoyed reading because that spoils it." People who can say this at least have started to develop a real appreciation for literature, and some are very perceptive readers indeed. But for a variety of reasons they are reluctant to examine their responses very closely. Sometimes this is due just to shyness or the fear of disapproval. But the most important reason seems to be the feeling that to criticize a work is to take all the life and fun out of it, like pulling apart a flower at the petals or trying to explain a good joke.

With experience you will find that the better you become at analysis the more enjoyable literature is. If you approach it in the right spirit, analysis will not destroy your appreciation of literature but enhance and deepen it, just as your appreciation for anything else is likely to increase as you come to understand how it works.

To begin with, try to go through a literary work you intend to analyze *twice over*, once for enjoyment, then for understanding. Don't try to become instantly analytical by making your first reading of a new work a painfully attentive effort. With practice analysis will become instinctive; for now, a two-stage reading process will be the best way both to preserve your spontaneous enjoyment of literature and help you to learn the necessary critical methods and tools.

Secondly, try to think of analysis not as an ordeal but as a game. In fact, think of the whole creative process as a game, a game of language, ideas, references, sounds, and patterns, a game in which the goal is to select, combine, and arrange these elements in ways that are as original, ambitious, and beautiful as possible. I do not mean to imply that literature should be thought of as some trivial pastime. Writing and criticism are not games in the sense of fooling around, but in the sense of a contest, seriously entered into, which requires a considerable amount of training and discipline beforehand but also the spirit of play. Partly they can be thought of as a challenging form of recreation like chess or figure skating or the decathlon, partly as resembling more serious kinds of mental play, like architectural design or city planning, which have greater intellectual significance and social consequences than most games but also involve the creative exercise of the imagination within a set of givens or rules.

As with any challenging game, the "rules" of literature allow great freedom for initiative and improvisation on the part of the individual writer or critic. As far as the writer is concerned, one could say that every literary form, and in a sense every individual work, is in fact a different game, the rules of which are determined by the author. He has total control over his choice of form, and once it is chosen he may alter it almost at will. If he is a poet, he may choose a strict form, like the sonnet, the conventions of which require him to write fourteen lines of ten-syllable rhyming verse, or he may choose an open form, like free verse, for which there is no predetermined pattern whatsoever. But even if he chooses the sonnet there are an infinite number of strategies he can use to get from the first word to the last.

The critic is somewhat more limited than the author, being bound (at least in theory) by the obligation to interpret the author's work. Yet the critic, too, is virtually unrestricted in his method of discussing his subject—a fact which once inspired the novelist Saul Bellow to describe criticism as "a rival form of imaginative literature." In the final analysis, criticism is not a set of routines which high school and college students are annually forced to rehearse, but simply the art of asking and discussing interesting questions about literature—questions which are interesting both to the critic and his audience. The number of such questions is really unlimited; some works will of course inspire more than others, but a truly inquisitive mind will be able to raise knotty questions about any piece of writing, even a ditty like:

> Mary had a little lamb,
> Its fleece was white as snow;
> And everywhere that Mary went
> The lamb was sure to go!
>
> It followed her to school one day,
> That was against the rule;
> It made the children laugh and play
> To see a lamb at school.
>
> And so the teacher turned it out,
> But still it lingered near;
> And waited patiently about
> Till Mary did appear.
>
> "Why does the lamb love Mary so?"
> The eager children cry;
> "Why Mary loves the lamb, you know!"
> The teacher did reply.

Does that one stump you? Well, here are some points to think about. (1) In addition to being a silly jingle, is the poem also, in a lighthearted way, contrasting the freedom and purity of nature with the rigidness of society, as personified by the schoolmaster? Does that help account for the poem's appeal to young children? (2) At the end of the poem, are we to believe that Mary has really triumphed over the schoolmaster by warming his heart? Or is the ending rather a sign that business is going on as usual, with question-and-answer drill between pupils and teacher? (Note that the authority figure gets the last word.) (3) Why should Mary be given a lamb for a pet, rather than, say, a dog or a cat? Is there any relevance to the fact that the lamb is a conventional symbol of Jesus and that Mary was Jesus's mother? Not that this is a deliberate religious reference, but mightn't it reveal something unconsciously about the attitudes of the author and her society?

To pursue these questions at any length would be paying quite a compliment to a piece of literary trivia. But if for some reason you did decide to study it closely, you would find that they raise rather complicated issues about the poem, its author, the times in which it was written, and its popularity. You would, in other words, have to call into play all four of the critical approaches discussed in the last chapter.

To be successful at criticism it is not enough, of course, simply to know you can ask any number of questions about a literary work. You also need to become familiar with the range of techniques and strategies which writers generally use, and with the range of questions which critics generally raise about them. Only after you have gained a sense of these can you really expect to become an insightful and creative reader, just as your body must develop another set of instincts if you are to become a skater or a dancer. The freedom I have described as belonging to the writer and critic comes only after practice. If, for example, you were to argue that "Mary Had a Little Lamb" is really a religious poem, your teacher would turn you out too. The idea has to be stated much more cautiously; with just the right degree of skepticism and perhaps a bit of humor besides.

The rest of the chapter will try to set you on the way to achieving that skill by outlining some of the most important things to look for when reading a literary work.

## READING FOR IMPLICATIONS

To begin with, you should have read the work attentively enough to get a sense of what it means on the *literal level—* that is, its surface meaning from passage to passage. Don't read Shakespeare so hastily that you interpret Hamlet's wish that "the Everlasting had not fixed his canon 'gainst self-slaughter" as implying that God is pointing a gun at him. Occasionally the style of a work is so obscure that even the surface meaning is unclear. Chapter Five will suggest some special ways of dealing with such works. But usually you can grasp at least the general drift.

Once you have arrived at this basic understanding, then you can start looking at the things which cannot be captured in a summary or paraphrase. These are the really important things about the work. Robert Frost once remarked that poetry is the part of a poem which can't be paraphrased, and the same could be said of all other literature. Indeed, the basic quality which makes a piece of writing more or less literary, as we saw in Chapter One, is an interest in the style or expression of the piece for its own sake, above and beyond a merely functional interest in what one has to say. To put this another way, creative writers are fond of indirection, of implying what they mean rather than telling it directly, or of suggesting a range of possible meanings. "Tell all the truth, but tell it slant," advises poet Emily Dickinson: "Success in Circuit lies."

You may sometimes think that the writer who does this is simply showing off, or trying to trick the reader; but this is usually not his major purpose, though it may very well be a part. More likely, the author's indirectness is rather an acknowledgement of the fact that most subjects which are important enough to write about are so complex and many-sided that one can't do justice to them by treating them in an explicit, definite way. This is especially true if the subject is an emotion or subjective experience. Take, for instance, these lines used by the poet W.B. Yeats to describe the workings of a mind of genius:

> Like a long-legged fly upon the stream
> His mind moves upon silence.

Yeats *could* have said something more straightforward, like "His mind moves in sudden unexpected leaps, when everything is silent." But the way he does express this general idea succeeds much better in capturing the actual feeling of the mysteriousness of the creative process. For instance, Yeats's lines suggest both a sense of the precariousness of the thought process and a sense of the mind's mastery over the outside forces which seem so much stronger than it. We half expect the insect to be drowned, but somehow it stays afloat and perhaps even makes headway against the stream. Notice too that Yeats avoids calling the long-legged fly a "waterbug," which would be much more colloquial and direct. Not only does this particular indirection have the effect of emphasizing the key part of the bug's anatomy, it also contributes to the general feeling of mystery. We see the action of the bug, like that of the mind, indistinctly. To describe either too literally would be to imply a sureness of knowledge about the creative process which we do not have.

It would not be correct, in most cases, to say that the creative writer makes a deliberate choice to express himself indirectly because he feels what he has to say is too complicated to say in plain, denotative language. Usually the reverse is true: he starts with a general commitment to expression in the form of stories, plays, poems, or whatever inspirations come to him. It may not occur to him to think, "Now I am going to be straightforward" or "Now I am going to be indirect." His concern, rather, is simply to realize his inspiration as fully as possible in the literary work. But the measure of his success at this, as in the Yeats passage, is, so to speak, the untranslatableness of the work: that is, the sense that no written explanation or paraphrase could serve as a substitute for the work itself. This does not mean that in order to be considered successful, literature must always deal with strange and obscure subjects like the mind of genius or make extensive use of tactics so offbeat as the comparison of the imagination to a waterbug. Consider the following lines from Shakespeare, for example:

> That time of year thou mayst in me behold
> When yellow leaves, or none, or few, do hang
> Upon those boughs which shake against the cold,
> Bare ruind choirs* where late the sweet birds sang.

*"Choirs" seems designed to suggest both "choirstalls" (of a ruined church) and the bird-like choir singers themselves.

The idea here is obvious: "I am growing old." The comparisons of aging to autumn and to a ruined building are also quite familiar. The artistry comes rather in the way the picture of the bare trees and the decrepit church are run together and made to suggest the body of a trembling old man, and in the unusual order of the items in the second line (yellow-none-few), which suggests the confusion and haltingness of an aging man's perceptions. Shakespeare's general idea here is easier to summarize than Yeats's, but it would be almost as hard to reduce these four lines to plain prose.

If literature succeeds to the extent that it resists paraphrase, a piece of criticism succeeds to the extent that it does justice to the subtlety and elusiveness of the works it discusses. Your first job as a critic, therefore, is to make yourself aware of the suggestiveness of the work you are reading. Here are some particular points to notice.

1. *Diction.* Be aware of the *connotations* or special implications of words. For Yeats, "Long-legged fly" and "waterbug" might have the same *denotation*—that is they refer to the same insect—but their connotations are very different. Can you see why "hang" is a better word for Shakespeare than "remain" or "cling"?

Also beware of possible *ambiguity,* or multiple meanings. Dickinson's "circuit," for example, means not only indirection alone but also completing the circle so as to capture or enclose the inspiration you set out to express. One of the favorite games in modern literature especially is to achieve as much ambiguity or multiplicity as possible.

Often the different connotations of a word or phrase are in *tension* with each other, forming a *paradox,* as with Yeats's long-legged fly, which is both puny and masterful. A good way to begin analyzing the connotations of a passage which seems ambiguous is to look for paradoxes, or opposites balanced against each other.

2. *Images.* An image is a verbal picture or representation which appeals to one or more of the senses. Shakespeare's boughs and choirs are images of aging, for example. Images are another basic form of literary indirection. Indeed the concept of image is so basic that the term is often used in a way that is virtually meaningless; for example, a Dickens novel might be spoken of as an "image"

of Victorian society. But in its more technical sense, the word refers to the use of vivid, sensuous language. In reading literature which is strongly imagistic, you should ask, "What do the images contribute to the total effect? How would it be if they were left out?" Think of all the other images Shakespeare could have used: a burnt-out volcano, a wilting flower, a crooked stick, old wine, a family heirloom, a faded tapestry.

3.   *Figurative Language—Metaphor—Imagery.* Metaphor is another term which is used ambiguously. (Indeed you'll find that the terminology of literary criticism can be almost as ambiguous as literature itself.) In its most restricted sense, metaphor refers to a particular kind of literary comparison in which two different things are directly equated with each other: "a boy's will is the wind's will," "life's but a walking shadow." Strictly speaking, "My love is like a red, red rose" is called a *simile,* or a likening, whereas "My love is a red, red rose" would be a metaphor. However, the term metaphor is often much more broadly used to refer to all figurative language (also called *imagery*): that is, any way of talking about one thing in terms of another. The category of figurative language or metaphor in the broad sense includes, among other things, images which are used for the purpose of illustration (as in both the Shakespeare and Yeats poems) rather than for purely narrative or descriptive reasons.

The various kinds of figurative language are defined in more detail in the other books in this series. For present purposes, we need only think of metaphor in general terms, as a sign of the fondness of writers for drawing analogies between one thing and another. Indeed this is such a common literary game, especially in poems, that some critics have even gone so far as to call metaphor the most essential characteristic of poetry. Although this may be an exaggeration, there is no doubt that one test of a creative imagination is its ability to see resemblances between disparate things. The following passage from Ralph Waldo Emerson is an example:

> there is no word in our language that cannot
> become typical to us of Nature by giving it emphasis.
> The world is a Dancer; it is a Rosary; it is a
> Torrent; it is a Boat; a Mist; a Spider's Snare;
> it is what you will; and the metaphor will hold,
> and it will give the imagination keen pleasure.

Emerson is often called a philosopher, but the delight and quickness with which his mind spins off these metaphors shows that he was also a poet. The private notebooks of other writers often reveal the same fondness for recording lists of images or metaphors or possible fictional situations. The good critic, by the same token, will train himself to notice not only the use of metaphor in the literature he reads, but also resemblances between authors, between different works by the same author, and between passages within the same work.

4. *The Larger Dimension: Symbolism, Allegory, Allusion, Archetype.* A *symbol* is a particular type of metaphor in which an image is said or implied to have a further significance. In the Emerson passage, the Dancer and the Rosary are symbols of nature; in the Yeats passage the fly symbolizes the operation of the mind, while the stream may be symbolic not only of silence but also of the flow of thought and/or time. As these examples suggest, the meaning of a symbol may either be simple and obvious or multiple and indefinite. An extreme example of the latter would be Melville's white whale, Moby-Dick, which has been variously interpreted as symbolizing God, the devil, nature, chaos, the forces of the unconscious, the repressive Puritan conscience, the monster Typhon in

Egyptian mythology, and the group of northern politicians who compromised with southern pro-slavery interests, including Melville's father-in-law. Critics frequently differentiate between such open-ended works, where the implied meanings are indefinite, and those where the action can be reduced to a clear-cut parable (like *Pilgrim's Progress* or William Golding's novel *Lord of the Flies)*, by calling the former *symbolic* and the latter *allegorical.*

An *allusion* is an explicit or implied reference to a particular person, place, event, or concept in history or legend. The title of Joyce's *Ulysses* is an obvious example; so are Melville's references to various events in the history of whaling during the course of *Moby Dick.* An *archetype* is a general image or situation or syndrome which because of its frequent recurrence over a period of time appears to be more or less universal in human experience. Shakespeare's comparison of aging to autumn is an example of an *archetypal image.* Conflict between different generations, the quest for an ideal paradise, and the "eternal triangle" of three jealous lovers are *archetypal situations,* while Don Juan and Oedipus might be said to be *archetypal characters,* in the sense that versions of them recur again and again in literature.

Symbolism and allegory, allusion and archetype are important to creative writers as ways of suggesting a larger dimension to the particular situation being described. Writers and critics alike are fond of drawing such analogies, partly because it is a pleasure and a challenge to do so, and partly because it heightens the significance—or at least the complexity—of the work. Melville, for instance, was determined that *Moby Dick* was not going to be about an ordinary whale.

On the other hand, he would undoubtedly have been distressed by some of the more far-out critical interpretations of what his book is about. In particular, Melville would have been irritated by the argument that *Moby Dick* "really" has nothing to do with whaling at all but is purely a symbolic work, for Melville himself had an ex-sailor's keen interest in the art of whaling in all its details. Particularly among inexperienced readers, what is called criticism all too often turns into a literary detective-hunt for "hidden meanings," the result of which usually reveals more about the critic's desire to be clever than about the work itself. Partly for this reason, authors have often been negative or aloof when questioned about hidden meanings in their works. Mark Twain's humorous preface to *Huckleberry Finn* warns readers not to look for a moral in his story upon pain of banishment. This warning should not be taken too seriously, however. In all probability Twain intended the novel to be more than just an entertaining story; and even if he didn't, the fact remains that it wound up (like any literary work) meaning more than the author intended. When you read *Huckleberry Finn,* for example, notice the contrast between the comical last section, where Huck is planning Jim's escape, and the rather more serious description of their trip down river; the contrast points to an important and unresolved conflict in the mind of the author between deeply pessimistic impulses and the desire to maintain an essentially optimistic, comic view of life. "Trust the tale, not the teller," as D.H. Lawrence advises.

Writers who discourage their audiences from looking for hidden meanings, then, should not be taken at face value. They, too, may very well believe that their work has a larger intellectual significance. But naturally they want it to be appreciated first of all for its own sake and not just as a symbol of something. The critic should approach the work in the same spirit. First get the feel of the poem or story or play; then think about what its further implications might be.

5. *Tone.* Anything you might think or say about the preceding topics should take into account the *tone* of the work, or the attitude conveyed by the work. In the passages on pp. 40, 41, and 44 you should note that Yeats is solemnly reflective, Shakespeare melancholy, Emerson is exhuberant. These tones are easy to grasp. Somewhat more complicated, however, is the beginning of Jane Austen's *Pride and Prejudice:*

> It is a truth universally acknowledged, that a single man in possession of a good fortune must be in want of a wife.

Here the tone is different from what one may at first think. The narrator is not stating her own view, as we soon find, but poking fun at neighborhood busybodies by stating their idle dreams in the dignified form of a universal maxim. Sometimes the tone is so complicated that one wonders if the author himself is sure of his thoughts about his subject. Take, for instance, Melville's description of one of the main characters in his short novel *Billy Budd:*

> Captain the Honorable Edward Fairfax Vere, to give his full title, was a bachelor of forty or thereabouts, a sailor of distinction even in a time prolific* of renowned seamen. Though allied to the higher nobility, his advancement had not been altogether owing to influences connected with that circumstance. He had seen much service, been in various engagements, always acquitting himself as an officer mindful of the welfare of his men, but never tolerating an infraction of discipline; thoroughly versed in the science of his profession, and intrepid to the verge of temerity, though never injudiciously so.

*Prolific – numerous.

Is Melville here describing the ideal officer, or is he damning Vere with faint praise? Is Vere's full title meant to sound impressive or stuffy? Should we conclude that he rose from the ranks mostly on his own merits, or because of personal influence? Does he have the right attitude toward his men, or is his sense of discipline excessive? Is he really brave, or is he essentially timid? Critics of Melville have debated these questions for decades, and they will continue to be debated. All that is certain about the passage is that Melville makes it impossible for the reader to draw an easy conclusion about Vere.

In many works the tone will be simple and straight-forward; in some, like *Billy Budd*, it may be one of the most difficult and interesting features of the author's style. In any case, you should always note the author's tone because it will determine your understanding of whatever he says and does. Is the work essentially serious or playful? Can you take what is said seriously, or is it *ironic*—that is, does it mean something quite different from what is actually said? Much of the effect of any criticism you may write will depend upon your tone, too. For example, the difference between the right and the wrong way of talking about the possible symbolism of "Mary Had a Little Lamb" is entirely a difference in tone. If you indicate that you are not taking the idea, or the poem, too seriously you will succeed; if you labor solemnly over the resemblances between the lamb and Christ, you will be sure to fail.

By now you have a better understanding of the reason for calling analysis a game, to be engaged in seriously yet also in the spirit of play. So much of literature is tentative, so much is left to implication, that good criticism must be tentative and flexible also. Otherwise it is going to be unfaithful to the spirit of the work.

Not that you should take this advice as meaning

"anything goes," however. It is absurd to claim that one interpretation is just as good as another. True, a number of works like *Moby Dick* are indeed so rich (and confusing) in their implications that you may well decide after reading them that almost anything might be said about them and made to stick somehow. But some hypotheses are clearly more probable than others, even though they cannot be proved in the same way as a mathematical theorem; and by the same token, it is easy to rule out certain literary interpretations as irrelevant, such as a claim that Yeats' fly "really" symbolizes the devil Beelzebub (whose name means "lord of the flies") or that Shakespeare's poem is about the beauty of autumn. The alternative interpretations of *Moby Dick* could be quickly divided by a group of intelligent readers into the two categories of "important" and "incidental." Beyond that, readers might start to disagree with each other about priorities, but it would not be a matter of arguing whether a religious interpretation is true or untrue, but of asking "How true is it?" At this point, there is still ample room for reasonable people to disagree without debating whether *any*thing true or false can be said about the book.

In literature, as in all fields of study, there is always room for new truth. As noted earlier, even ancient classics are still being revalued and reinterpreted. But this doesn't mean everything that was previously said about them is or should be discarded every time. In the long run, the flexibility and openendedness of literature and criticism should encourage you to exercise your creativity (as well as your caution), rather than make you feel anxious or cynical about the possibility of saying anything meaningful about the work.

## READING FOR PATTERNS

In analyzing literature you need to look not only for the different kinds of implications suggested on the previous pages but for patterns running through the work as a whole. The analytical approach to criticism, you will recall, assumes that a work has *coherence,* that the various parts relate to each other in forming a unified whole. This assumption clearly works much better for some types of literature than for others; for example, short lyric poems are as a rule more tightly unified than novels. Sometimes, indeed, it is important for a work to be rather incoherent, as in some types of comic narrative where a rambling quality is essential to the overall effect. Still, a good writer will maintain control over his subject even when it is in his interest to ramble; and unless you can prove otherwise, it is only fair to assume that the author of the work you are criticizing knew exactly what he was doing. One of the chief ways of seeing and testing this control in practice is by looking for the following patterns.

1. *Recurring Elements: Motifs, Themes, Parallels.* A *motif* is a word, phrase, action, or idea which is repeated during the course of a work. Sometimes a motif is simply a shorthand way of setting a tone or establishing a character, such as in Dickens' *A Christmas Carol,* where Ebenezer Scrooge's "Bah! Humbug!" quickly types him as a Christmas-hater. But a motif can also have more extensive, complicated symbolic overtones. In *Hamlet,* for example, poisoning and disguise are rather complicated motifs, involving a number of characters and situations and suggesting not only the treachery of the king's court but also Hamlet's inevitable entrapment in these evils as he seeks to clear his father's name.

If the recurring feature is a major part of the work, like revenge and kinship in *Hamlet,* it is usually called a *theme*. This term is also used to denote what is taken to be the most central action or idea of a work, as when we say "the theme of John Milton's *Paradise Lost* is the fall of Adam and Eve," or "Hawthorne's theme in *The Scarlet Letter* is that sin is compounded when it is not confessed."

Perhaps the best way to begin to grasp the themes of a relatively long and complicated work and the manner in which they are put together is to look for *parallels* or analogies between different characters, events, and situations. Take *The Scarlet Letter*, for instance. This book has four main characters: Hester Prynne, a Puritan woman; her former lover Dimmesdale, the local minister; their illegitimate child, Pearl; and Hester's former husband Chillingsworth, who is something of a cross between a scholar and a sorcerer. The main action proceeds as follows. Pearl is born at the outset; neither parent reveals who the father is, so Hester is ostrasized by the community, while Dimmesdale remains untouched by suspicion in his position as the local spiritual leader. Chillingsworth, however, resolves to find out the secret; and he does, by worming his way into intimacy with Dimmesdale. But his singleminded obsession with revenge turns him into something of a monster in the process. Pearl's life is also somewhat strained by having to grow up without a father in isolation from society; she is both Hester's sole consolation and her trial, by constantly asking her "Who is my father?" Even so, Hester is, in a way, better off than Dimmesdale, because her guilt is exposed and she is gradually forgiven by the townspeople; whereas Dimmesdale suffers from remorse at his own hypocrisy and slowly wastes away. Finally, Dimmesdale and Hester resolve to run away from the community altogether; but when their escape is threatened by Chillingsworth, Dimmesdale, feeling that he is about to die, reveals himself to the townspeople; and father, mother, and child are at least momentarily united in public before Dimmesdale expires. Now that the truth is revealed, Pearl instantly changes from a disturbed, almost devilish child into a normal young woman.

As you read through this story, you begin to see that the characters are related and contrasted to each other in a number of different ways. All four suffer from the effects of secrecy. But Hester and Pearl remain essentially intact because their guilt has been revealed, while Dimmesdale and Chillingsworth destroy themselves from within even though they look respectable from without. Again, Chillingsworth and Pearl play somewhat parallel roles in serving both as friend and torturer to Dimmesdale and Hester. Dimmesdale and Chillingsworth are also paralleled as the two men in Hester's life; both also happen to be intellectual, bookish, devious men. (One wonders what Hester saw in them! This is a typical Hawthorne pattern, incidentally: the beautiful, vibrant woman coupled with an introverted and often listless male.) Dimmesdale and Chillingsworth also occupy symbolic roles in the community, as minister (spiritual healer) and doctor (physical healer), but Hester successfully competes with them as a kind of informal social worker.

Many other such parallels and contrasts could be drawn between the four characters, to the point that the reader begins to see Hawthorne almost as a kind of mathematician or juggler, engaged in an elaborate balancing act. Many other creative writers also love to treat their chosen themes in a variety of ways during the course of a work, multiplying, comparing, and contrasting. Very rarely does one find these parallels laid out with the symmetry of a geometrical design; more often they involve a good deal of improvisation, which the writer later tightens up to some degree in the process of revision. Nor is it likely that he is conscious of all the analogies and echoes between different parts of the work. But unquestionably he is aware to some degree; his mind is moving along certain lines; and the result is the kind of patterning which has just been noted in *The Scarlet Letter.* As you read any literary work, you should look for and expect to find a network of such patterns. In some writing, they will be as simple as the good guy in the white hat vs. the villain with the black moustache, the girl next door vs. the exotic temptress, and the like. But in serious literature they will be highly complex and sophisticated.

2. *Structure.* The overall design or organization of the work is generally called its *structure.* The structure is, so to speak, the skeleton of the work, in contrast to what is sometimes called its *texture,* namely the style or flow or "feel" of the work from passage to passage. The notion of structure includes the kinds of patterns previously discussed, in the sense that they contribute toward the shaping of the action into a coherent whole. Any feature of a work which helps to control its organization may be considered as a part of its structure.

A particular work can be structured in one or more of several ways. A play or story will have a *narrative structure* or *plot*—that is, an overall pattern to the action to which all the details are more or less subordinate, like the pattern of revenge in *Hamlet* or the pattern of sin and penitence in *The Scarlet Letter.* In essays as well as in poetry, drama, and narrative which is strongly philosophical or reflective, a *thematic structure* will be the main organizing principle. In such cases, if the work is strongly didactic the structure will consist of the elaboration of an argument; if it is primarily lyric, then the structure will consist of the elaboration of an emotion through its various stages. An example which falls in between these two extremes is the

Shakespeare sonnet of which the first four lines were quoted on page 41.

> That time of year thou mayst in me behold
> When yellow leaves, or none, or few, do hang
> Upon those boughs which shake against the cold,
> Bare ruin'd choirs where late the sweet birds sang.
> In me thou seest the twilight of such day
> As after sunset fadest in the west,
> Which by and by black night doth take away,
> Death's second self, that seals up all in rest.
> In me thou seest the glowing of such fire,
> That on the ashes of his youth doth lie,
> As the death-bed whereon it must expire,
> Consumd with that which it was nourish'd by.
>    This thou perceiv'st, which makes thy love more strong,
>    To love that well which thou must leave ere long.*

*The line literally means "to love well him whom you will soon be leaving." The speaker pictures himself on his death bed, with the friend saying a last farewell to him.

On the surface, the poem is presented in the form of a logical argument, addressed to a second person: because you see me growing old, your love becomes stronger, for you know I'll soon be gone. (One wonders, incidentally, just how sure the speaker is of the friend's love; if so, why does he need to make this assertion?) But the reader should quickly see that Shakespeare's interest is not so much in the proposition itself as in the elaboration of the metaphors of dying: that is, the comparisons of dying with fall, sunset, and the fading fire. Notice that these three images form a sequence. First, the references to death become increasingly more explicit with each image. Autumn simply reminds one of old age, sunset is a direct anticipation of death, the fading fire actually seems like a deathbed. Secondly, and more abstractly, the progression involves a narrowing focus: autumn is part of the cycle of the year, sunset part of the cycle of a day, the fire exhausts itself in a few hours; also, the first two cycles renew themselves, the last does not.

There is also a *prosodic or verse structure* in Shakespeare's poem, of course. Each of the three images is developed within one four-line rhyming unit, and the conclusion is given in a separate couplet.

Once it starts to become second nature to detect such patterns in literature, you will find that they become a great source of stimulation and enjoyment. Not that most literary works, including Shakespeare's, are structured so precisely. In most of Shakespeare's 154 sonnets, for example, the divisions in the rhyme do not correspond so closely with the division in meaning. And it is good that this is so, for preciseness is only one way of measuring quality in literature, and one would quickly grow tired reading only works of that kind. As noted above, some types of writing need to be relatively unstructured in order to achieve a particular effect. But even in those cases, you should expect to find a sort of organizational design. *Stream-of-consciousness* writing, the literary imitation of the actual process of thought, for example, is often unified by the use of recurring motifs, which indicate the special preoccupations of the person who is thinking and help to establish his character.

In all good literature, there is an interrelationship between *form* and *content,* between what the author says and the way he has to say it: a particular story, poem, or play will tend to take shape in a given way, and the shape it takes will in turn both heighten and limit the main features of the work. In *The Scarlet Letter,* for example,

Hawthorne uses very little dialogue; his favorite approach is to concentrate on the inner life of each character in turn. This has the desired effect of emphasizing the isolation of the characters from each other, but similarly it prevents the reader from visualizing them as fully as characters in Jane Austen's novels, which are much more concerned with the interaction of people in social situations. As a result, group scenes are much more often pivotal in the structure of her novels than in Hawthorne's. When studying the structure of a given work, you should look for such relationships between form and content.

In most works, the structure will not be obvious, and in some it will be so unclear that not even discussion among professional critics can establish it. The basic reason for this is that although writers generally work from a vision of what the main outlines of their work should be, they do not usually think in terms of following a very particular 1—2—3 order as they are writing it; and even if they do, they usually try not to make the order too explicit, so as to preserve the illusion of naturalism and spontaneity. No skeleton key exists which will enable you to penetrate this illusion in all cases and see how a work is constructed. Often this knowledge comes very slowly, after a number of readings of a work in diverse moods. Even after prolonged study you will probably not discover anything as clear-cut as a blueprint or even a skeleton, but rather a set of more or less closely interrelated patterns which together help to control and give shape to the work.

Do not expect, then, to be able to reduce the structure of a complex work to a neat formula; but on the other hand always assume that there is more order to the work than you at first notice. Here are some general guidelines which may help you in your search. (a) Try to break down the main action or argument or sequence of thought into divisions or stages. Sometimes it even helps to draw a diagram. (b) Consider how the various recurring elements might fit into larger patterns—how, for example, the various child-parent relationships in *Hamlet* enter into the main action of Hamlet's delayed revenge. (c) Look for relationships between form and content. When you notice what is obviously a structural device, such as the rhyme scheme in Shakespeare's sonnet, consider how that particular device may be an appropriate way of organizing the author's meaning. (d) Reflect about any resemblances you may have detected between the work and other literary works, particularly those by the same author. After reading several of Hawthorne's stories, for example, one quickly begins to get a sense of how the typical Hawthorne tale is organized, and the same is true for most writers. But in addition to relying on their own previous inventions, authors also borrow a great deal, whether consciously or not, from literary tradition, as we shall see in the following section.

3. *Traditional Patterns: Genres, Conventions, Archetypal Situations.* A *genre* is a general literary category or type, like tragedy or comedy or epic, which has developed over the course of time. The conventions of epic, for example, include a lofty style, a hero of extraordinary abilities whose destiny is in some sense tied in with that of his whole nation, and the use of supernatural figures and events. Some genres, like the lyric, are miscellaneous and indefinite; some, like the sonnet (which is a type of lyric and therefore sometimes called a *sub-genre*) are very specific in their conventions. In the latter case, a knowledge of genres and conventions is of great help to the analyst. It helps to know, for instance, that *Hamlet* is a "revenge tragedy" and that revenge tragedies typically include the use of motifs like the ghost of the murdered man, the hesitation of the hero, real or pretended madness, and a

bloodbath at the end. Knowing that these devices are conventional can help one to understand some of the strange
twists in the play, as well as to appreciate the originality
with which Shakespeare puts these conventions to new
uses. The same is true for the poem discussed in the previous
section; it is written in the form we now call the *Shakes-
pearean sonnet.*

As you attempt to analyze a literary work, therefore,
you should consider not only its particular characteristics
but its genre—or its genres, for sometimes a work is a
mixture of several. Sometimes the work will be so atypical
or the genre so vague that your reflections will be of no
extra help, but sometimes they will clarify your understanding a great deal. In the other books in this series,
much more will be said about the conventions of the various
genres of poetry, drama, and the narrative to help you in
this undertaking.

Whether or not a work falls into a distinct literary
genre, its structure may rely heavily upon particular conventions or archetypes, and it is important to look for them
too. Perhaps the best way to understand the structure of
*The Scarlet Letter,* for example, is in terms of the archetypal religious cycle of sin-suffering-repentance-redemption.
A more modern archetype which influences the structure
of a number of American literary works, like Arthur Miller's
*Death of a Salesman,* is the American dream of success as
available to every individual. Again, you will often find the
conventions of the epic both adapted and parodied (in
what is called *mock-epic)* in modern literature. The char-
acterization of Leopold Bloom in Joyce's *Ulysses* is a case
in point. To be able to identify such ways in which writers
make use of traditional patterns will not only help you to
understand how the work is organized but also, in many
cases, give you an important clue to the tone and leading

ideas of the work. Miller's play, for example, must be understood in part as a criticism of the American dream; Joyce's novel is partly serio-comic commentary on the shabbiness of the present as contrasted with our vision of the heroic past.

You should not be expected to be able to detect many of these generic, conventional, and archetypal patterns until you have read a good deal of literature. Nor in any case should you look to them as providing all the solutions to all your remaining questions about a work. Any good work is only typical to a certain degree. A good deal of *Hamlet* will remain a mystery even after one has mastered the conventions of revenge tragedy. Still, an awareness of these larger patterns will definitely enrich your understanding of what you read and make your analysis much more enjoyable and challenging.

A great deal more could be said about the methods of literary analysis. But the outline just given will provide you with at least a basic framework for understanding and talking about these and all other kinds of writing. Rather than go into further detail about the analytical approach to literature, therefore, let us now try to apply it and the three other critical approaches to a particular example.

# CHAPTER FOUR

# THE FOUR CRITICAL APPROACHES IN ACTION

For the sake of convenience, let us use a short poem to illustrate the four major approaches to literature: "A Noiseless Patient Spider," by Walt Whitman. It isn't a flawless poem—the diction is heavy and abstract—but it is a good poem, as well as a good example for our purposes. It is easy to understand in a general way, and yet it presents some complicated and interesting problems of interpretation.

### A NOISELESS PATIENT SPIDER

A noiseless patient spider,
I mark'd where on a little promontory it stood isolated,
Mark'd how to explore the vacant vast surrounding,
It launch'd forth filament, filament, out of itself,
Ever unreeling them, ever tirelessly speeding them.

And you, O my soul, where you stand,
Surrounded, detached, in measureless oceans of space,
Ceaselessly musing, venturing, throwing, seeking the
                              spheres to connect them,
Till the bridge you will need be form'd, till the ductile
                              anchor hold,
Till the gossamer thread you fling catch somewhere,
                    O my soul.

## THE ANALYTICAL APPROACH

As noted earlier, the process of analysis is a process of gradually collecting and refining your thoughts about a work over a period of time. But you might think of the process as having two main steps: the first is to grasp a general sense of the main stylistic features of the work; the second is to criticize and question that general impression until you are sure that it is as thorough and as precise as possible.

*Stage one.* Perhaps the first thing you will notice is that the poem is built around two parallel images which are joined together to form one metaphor, the comparison of the spider with the speaker's soul. The structure of the poem as a whole is fairly obvious. Although it is written in "free verse," with no definite pattern of rhythm or rhyme, the poem is rather tightly organized into two *stanzas,* or line-groupings, of equal number and approximately equal length. The stanzas each begin with relatively short lines describing the central object, becoming longer as the action is described.

The general meaning of the metaphor should also become evident upon the first reading. Spider and soul resemble each other in being persistent, quiet, tiny in the face of "the vacant vast surrounding," isolated but seeking in different ways to make contact with what is around them. The poem suggests that this may be a difficult task: the filaments are fragile and the spider/soul must keep throwing them out again and again. But the poem is not exactly pessimistic, either; one feels that the spider/soul will keep trying until they are successful.

All this is conveyed directly or indirectly by the language of the poem, especially the adjectives and verbs. Unlike the excerpts from Yeats and even Shakespeare, the images are not obscure, nor is the language particularly difficult, ambiguous, or even unusual. Except for the beautiful word "ductile," which suggests both the tenuousness and the inner strength of the soul's filaments, the language is quite ordinary.*

If you are reasonably well-read, you might also notice that the features of Whitman's poem are derived from literary tradition. The qualities of the spider, for example, are conventional. In general, several different archetypal spiders appear in English and American writing: the devilish spider which spins webs like Satan to catch poor mortals; the artistic spider, whose webs are compared to the subtlety of art; and the noiseless patient variety, whose usual function is to remind the observer of the virtue of perseverance. If the poem makes you think about these conventions, so much the better; if it doesn't, no great harm is done. They are not essential to the appreciation of the poem.

You have now developed a good working notion of the poem's structure, main techniques, and basic meaning. But if you are now satisfied that you "understand" the poem, that is because you haven't really looked for anything difficult. Look again at the ground you have just covered and you may have some second thoughts.

*Stage two.* You might begin by asking why Whitman chose the particular structure he did, rather than another. In other words, what is the relationship between form and content here? What is the contribution of the structure to the total effect of the poem? You may now begin to

---

*Much more could be said about the poem's language and images than is discussed in this chapter. Notice, for example, the various words and phrases which have to do with the sea and voyages: promontory, launch'd, oceans of space, the ductile anchor. Whitman was very fond of the metaphor of the soul's quest as a voyage and to a certain extent this poem reflects that interest.

see a symbolic appropriateness in Whitman's having developed his two images in isolation from each other: isolation is also the problem which soul and spider have to surmount. The isolation of spider and soul is emphasized by the structure of the poem. Each is "isolated" at the outset of the stanza; and the progressively lengthier lines which follow suggest the attempts of both soul and spider to reach out beyond themselves. Finally, the contrast between the neatness of the parallel organization of the stanzas and the disjointed restlessness of the rhythms ("Ceaselessly musing, venturing, throwing") emphasizes the contrast between the present uneasiness of soul and spider and the security they hope eventually to achieve.

As you become more aware of this contrast, you might want to reexamine the formulation of the poem's meaning proposed a moment ago. It is easy to see what the different connotations of the metaphor are, but what do they really add up to? What is the tone of the poem? Is it primarily optimistic, or is the primary tone rather one of restless uncertainty? The "vacant vast" and the "measureless oceans" surrounding soul and spider seem threatening rather than hospitable. In the last two lines, the progression of "bridge" to "ductile anchor" to "gossamer thread" suggests an ever-more tenuous and uncertain connection between the soul and its object. These hints imply a more sombre view of the poem, which the vague word "somewhere" in the last line does nothing to counteract. Not that the poem should be interpreted as an outcry of desperation; it is far from that. The point is simply that your first impression of its tone will probably be deceiving. The poem's neat organization and hopeful vision of the bridge and the anchor at first tempt you to feel more reassured than you should be. What is actually described in the poem is not how isolation is overcome so much as what it is like to be isolated.

Finally, you might ask yourself what is the soul looking for? What is that indefinite "somewhere"? Does it
refer to God, heaven, society, a friend or lover, its own
identity, or what? Or should the object simply be thought
of as indefinite, as applying to any kind of spiritual isolation? At this point, the other critical approaches begin to
enter into our picture, as we shall see in a moment, and a
variety of suggestions might be put forward as to what the
poem "really" means, none of which can really be proven,
but all of which have at least the merit of being provocative.
For example, a strictly analytical critic might wish to see
the spider as an artist-figure and the poem as a whole as a
parable of the difficulty of creating a coherent work of art
from the diverse and scattered materials which the poet
must bring together. This interpretation is rather shaky, because the poem is apparently concerned with a problem of
the spirit itself rather than a problem of craftsmanship; but
the two concerns are sufficiently related closely enough
(especially in the mind of the poet) that the interpretation
cannot be absolutely ruled out. It is at least an incidental
meaning, if not an important one.

In any case, it is striking that a poem which probably
strikes most readers as quite obvious upon first reading
should turn out, in the long run, to be rather elusive. Not
all literary works are similar in this respect, by any
means. Sometimes, for example, the reverse is true: a
work which seems very obscure at first turns out to
be rather shallow and perhaps just poorly written. But
in general you will find that there is more to serious
literature than you have at first noticed. As we go on
to see how "A Noiseless Patient Spider" might be interpreted in the light of the other major critical approaches,
the poem will come to seem even more many-sided
than we have just seen.

## THE MIMETIC APPROACH

From this point of view, the poem is especially significant as an expression of the spirit and values of its age. As a mimetic critic, you might wish to begin by connecting the fact that the poem was published shortly after the Civil War with its mood of personal and religious uncertainty. Whitman was writing in a period when most of the major American and British writers were undergoing a crisis of faith. Most were essentially serious-minded men, very concerned about religion, in search of a creed or ideal in which they could believe, but unable to accept traditional Christianity. Their writing tends to reflect this quest. The Civil War, in which Whitman was directly involved as a volunteer hospital worker, was an additional force in disturbing the settled convictions of American thinkers, both about their religion and their social order. With these facts in mind, you might wish to regard the soul-spider as an image of the spiritual predicament of the mid-nineteenth century mind in search of a secure faith in God, heaven, and an ordered universe.

Related to the general mood of spiritual uncertainty was a tendency, among writers of the period, to turn to nature for consolation and guidance. Whitman's poem reflects this also, not only in its content but also in its form. The two-stage process of describing a natural image and then relating it to the speaker's state of mind is a conventional approach in nature lyrics, especially during the Romantic period. For example, Whitman's contemporary William Cullen Bryant does the same thing in his poem, "To the Fringed Gentian." After describing the blossoming flower just before the onset of winter, Bryant concludes with this expression of hope:

> I would that thus, when I shall see
> The hour of death draw near to me,

> Hope, blossoming within my heart
> May look to heaven as I depart.

A mimetic critic would perhaps be more interested in the differences between Bryant and Whitman than in the similarities, however. He might note that the technique of free verse—of which Whitman was the earliest important pioneer in English poetry—is better suited than Bryant's form to the expression of the anxieties of the speaker as well as his hope. The regular, systematic beat of Bryant's verse exudes a kind of confidence and reassuringness which the speaker does not quite feel. The less structured form of Whitman's poem would be likely to interest the mimetic critic as a more faithful, though not so typical, representation of the spiritual reality which both poets had to face. Bryant's style would be likely to interest him in another way, as symptomatic of a more timid spirit trying to preserve itself intact by clinging to traditional forms.

The mimetic critic might also point to the same contradiction in Whitman, however. For even as "A Noiseless Patient Spider" professes ignorance of the measureless oceans of space, the level of realism on which Whitman writes is such as to encourage the belief in a meaningful universe. For example, nature is given a certain amount of consciousness: the spider is described partly in human terms—as "patient," as standing rather than crawling, as very observant, as an explorer. The soul, furthermore, is given a tangible reality in the second stanza. In other words, although on the surface the poem doesn't resolve the questions of whether the "somewhere" sought by soul and spider is a real place or just a "vacant vast," the poem is not atheistic or even agnostic. In its way of portraying spider and soul it quietly assumes the existence of a supernatural dimension to things. Some of the minor images in the poem reinforce this assumption: the bridge and the anchor, for example, are traditional symbols of religious faith. Altogether, then, a mimetic critic would find Whitman's poem, both in its style and in its content, a reflection of the transition between an earlier age of faith and our modern age of doubt.

## PRAGMATIC APPROACHES

If you approached the poem as a philosophical statement, you would agree with the mimetic critic that it describes the predicament of an individual in search of a secure and coherent world-view. But your interest would not be so much in the way this predicament is represented as in the way the poem puts forth an implied model of human conduct. You would notice that although no definite solution is presented to the problem facing the speaker, he does at least accept the method of the spider as a way of finding such a solution. Like the spider, the soul must patiently persevere, relying on its own resources to make the best of its situation. It might even occur to you to describe this poem as an anticipation of twentieth-century existentialism, as expressed in Camus's *The Myth of Sisyphus,* for example. In this work human effort is reduced to a cycle of frustration. Sisyphus, Camus's representative man, is condemned to push a huge rock up a hill in Hades, and to have the rock forever slip away and roll back down just before it gets to the top. The situation is not nearly so hopeless in Whitman's poem; it is entirely possible that the soul will eventually make the connection it seeks; but for the present, the only real alternative for it is to persist faithfully in its efforts despite continual defeat.

You would also be interested, as a philosophical or didactic critic, in seeing the poem as a reflection of Whitman's personal philosophy as a whole, and the way in which he believed this philosophy should affect his work.

You would note, for example, Whitman's repeated insistence that the essential purpose of his writing was to celebrate a new religion and life-style as exemplified by the portrayal of the actions and thoughts of a single ideal personality (modeled on himself), engaging in a great range of different activities. According to this notion as stated by Whitman himself, every poem he wrote might be considered as presenting a portion of a larger, systematic world-view. To know that Whitman felt this way would reinforce the idea that "A Noiseless Patient Spider" is really a statement of the proper way to respond to the problem of spiritual uncertainty.

As you continued to study Whitman's philosophical side, however, you would notice also that his poems as a whole are quite contradictory in the statements they make, and that they vary also in the degree to which they philosophize. This poem is much less didactic than many Whitman wrote; it is a "musing" or "venturing" (like the soul itself) rather than a preachment or moralization. It is significant that the poem ends with the poet addressing his soul, rather than the reader (as Whitman does in a number of other poems). You would have to conclude, therefore, that although the poem is philosophical, it is not actually didactic—it is not set up in such a way as to make the teaching of a lesson a primary part of its purpose.

If you approached the poem affectively, you would probably take special note in the way it partly resolves and partly stimulates the feelings of aimlessness and bewilderment through the use of free verse vs. unified structuring and the contrast between the present state and the future hopes of the soul/spider. Whitman's handling of both contrasts, you might observe, encourages the reader to admit his own doubts without feeling overwhelmed by them. It could be argued that the poem thereby has a therapeutic function for the anxious person who reads it, for the poem says, in effect: yes, the anxiety you feel about the uncertainty of things has a real basis; I have felt the same way also; you need not be ashamed of such emotions, nor need you feel trapped by them because without doubt they are part of some larger design which eventually you can hope to find, even though now it is not visible. Such a train of thought might at least temporarily relieve the mind of the reader who responded to it.

On the other hand, it could also be argued that the consolation is too easy, especially for a modern reader, who is less likely to believe in bridges and anchors of faith, who can spot the sentimentality of humanizing the spider as Whitman does. The affective critic might ultimately conclude, therefore, that the poem imposes a rationalizing solution on its subject too easily to permit a sensitive person to respond to it with any spontaneity.

In either case, however, the focus of discussion would be the question of the effect which the poem is likely to have on the reader. In pursuing this question the critic would probably try to distinguish and compare the poem's emotional impact and its intellectual impact. If the critic had a knowledge of clinical psychology, he might also try to trace in quite specific terms the possible impact of the poem's various elements on the reader's subconscious mind and their role in his overall response to the poem. Since my own knowledge of this field is very limited, I am not sure what conclusions he would draw; perhaps the metaphor of the soul as a small spider spinning in the void would suggest to him, among other things, the irrational defensive impulse to make oneself very tiny and obscure when confronted with much larger, more powerful forces.

## THE EXPRESSIVE APPROACH

From this point of view, you would regard the poem as an expression of the author's personality. You would proceed from the assumption that the soul/spider is an image of Whitman himself—not the whole man, perhaps, but nevertheless a window through which to view his character. You would, therefore, pay special attention to the circumstances under which the poem was composed, to possible ways in which it echoes or makes direct use of autobiographical episodes, and to any additional information which might be suggested by your general knowledge of psychology.

For example, you would be very interested to know that the original version of the poem, written some eight years before the final version was published, contains a number of self-revealing details which the later version omits:

> The Soul, reaching, throwing out for love,
> As the spider, from some little promontory, throwing
>    out filament after filament, tirelessly out of itself,
>    that one at least may catch and form a link, a
>    bridge, a connection
> O I saw one passing alone, saying hardly a word—yet
>    full of love I detected him, by certain signs
> O eyes wishfully turning! O silent eyes!
> For then I thought of you oer the world
> O latent oceans, fathomless oceans of love!
> O waiting oceans of love! yearning and fervid! and of
>    you sweet souls perhaps in the future, delicious
>    and long:
> But Dead, unknown on the earth—ungiven, dark here,
>    unspoken, never born:
> You fathomless latent souls of love—you pent and
>    unknown oceans of love!

Clearly, no one who becomes aware of the existence of

this early draft can then read the finished poem in quite the same way. Here the sea of faith is the sea of love, and the isolation referred to is not metaphorical isolation but the loneliness which the speaker sees in those (probably including himself) who are unfulfilled, who long for love and human contact. Further reading of Whitman's poetry reveals that a central theme is the celebration of and longing for male companionship, and that this theme probably reflected homosexual impulses which Whitman partly displayed and partly concealed. Bearing all this in mind, an expressivist critic might be tempted to conjecture that Whitman's original draft was inspired by a particular person or incident he observed. He may have later toned down the love-element and played up the spiritual element in order to be more discreet, but still meant the poem (for himself if not for the reader) to capture the problem of human communication rather than the search for philosophical certainty.

An analytic critic, on the other hand, would more likely take the view that Whitman simply discovered that the latter theme made a better poem than the communication theme, while a pragmatic critic might point out that the search for a faith motif became stronger in Whitman's thought as he grew older, displacing to some extent the theme of comradeship. Instead of looking for earthly comrades, Whitman turned his sights to what he called "the comrade perfect." Altogether then, the mere knowledge of the origins of the poem, even assuming that it was inspired by a true and specific incident (which it may not have been), is not sufficient to prove that the other interpretations are wrong. But it does suggest a good deal both about the way Whitman's imagination worked and the way writers in general tend to capitalize upon and transform highly personal feelings and events in the process of creating literature.

## CONCLUSIONS

This chapter has not tried to say everything which could be said about "A Noiseless Patient Spider," but simply to suggest the range of different ways in which you might approach it and any literary work you may study. As you pursue these approaches independently, bear in mind the following general points. (1) Not all are equally useful or interesting in a given case. For example, the expressive approach happens to be unusually rewarding for this particular poem, but it would be virtually useless for a work whose author is unknown. (2) Regardless of your topic, it is usually helpful to consider your general subject beforehand from several viewpoints. For example, a critic who argued that the spider symbolized the artist without bothering to take into account other possibilities would produce a very one-sided paper. (3) Conversely, it is unusually misleading to say that one of the basic critical approaches to this and other works is "wrong" while another is "right." An approach may be more or less fruitful, and more or less skillfully used in a given case, but the differences among approaches is a difference in what we are actually looking for in a given work rather than a difference between right and wrong. (4) Whatever your personal attitude towards these various approaches, begin by being an analytic reader: that is, read the work carefully, and try to figure out how it is put together before you do anything else with it. Otherwise, you may find yourself engrossed and adrift with your own pet theory, while the work itself is left far behind. But finally, (5) remember that ultimately there is more to literary appreciation than the analytical approach. Although most literature courses and handbooks, including this one, primarily emphasize how literature is put together, analytical criticism in itself can only capture a part of the reader's total response to a work. One of the major aims of Chapters Two and Four of this book has been to convey a fuller sense of the whole range of ways in which literature can be read and appreciated. It is important to regard analytical criticism not simply as an end in itself but also as an avenue to a deeper understanding of how a literary work serves as a testament of values, an expression of its author's personality, and an embodiment of its age.

# CHAPTER FIVE

# READING LITERATURE FROM DIFFERENT PERIODS

The two opposing schools of thought on the value of studying literary history can be summarized by the following statements: (1) good literature transcends the age in which it was written and appeals to readers in all ages; and (2) any literary work that is more than ten years old or so needs to be translated somewhat before we can understand it.

Both statements are true. On the one hand, nothing ages as rapidly as today's best-seller, while some unknown contemporary writers are sure to be recognized as classics a hundred years from now. By 1975, Barbara Carson's satire of Lyndon Johnson in *Macbird* will be forgotten (if it hasn't been already); but the original *Macbeth* will still be read annually by thousands of high school students. But on the other hand, these same students will have trouble understanding *Macbeth* without footnotes and explanations. Not only must the language in the play be annotated, it is also helpful to explain the attitudes toward witchcraft, royalty, and usurpation in Shakespeare's day, as well as the extent to which Macbeth fits the pattern of a particular kind of tragic hero in the drama of the period: the character who rises swiftly through good fortune but falls spectacularly through pride, overreaching, and misdeeds.

The scope of this book is too limited to include a

complete rundown on the whole course of English and American literary history, although the bibliography lists some works of that type, and the appendix gives a skeleton outline of the major periods of literary history. This chapter will focus upon some general ideas and hints as to how to overcome the feeling of strangeness upon first encountering literature from an unfamiliar period. Since a good deal of modern literature is as obscure, if not more so, than works of previous periods, this chapter will divide literary history into two main parts: literature before about 1900 and twentieth century literature.

## APPROACHING PRE-MODERN LITERATURE

1. *The Language Barrier.* The older the work, the more likely you are to get the impression that it is written in a foreign language. To read most medieval literature, like the poetry of Geoffrey Chaucer, the introductory student will even need a special dictionary, while writing from the Anglo-Saxon period (like the epic *Beowulf*) will seem quite unintelligible in the original. Fortunately, there are many annotated editions of all important older works, in which the most difficult words and passages are explained. But even so, you will sometimes be baffled or misled by the writer's language, such as when he uses a familiar word in an archaic sense. For example, in Andrew Marvell's seventeenth-century poem "To His Coy Mistress" the speaker swears that

> My vegetable love should grow
> Vaster than empires and more slow.

Before you conclude that his beloved is being compared with a cabbage, consult the *Oxford English Dictionary* (also called the *New English Dictionary*), which is the best guide to the history of the English language. Most libraries will have either the complete ten-volume version or the one-volume abridgment. It will suggest that "vegetable" is here being used as an adjective, in the outdated sense of "growing," like a vegetable.

Of course reading is not much fun when you must constantly consult footnotes or the dictionary. As a rule, this approach is advisable only when you feel you need these aids in order to understand the general drift of what you're reading, or when you encounter a seemingly strange usage in a passage which is necessary for you to understand precisely for purposes of analysis. In general, perhaps the best way to cope with the language barrier in a difficult work is to read a portion of it with great care, so that you get a fairly definite sense of the difficulties involved and what the characteristics of this strange new style are; and then read the remainder at your ordinary reading speed, avoiding inundation with the difficult words and passages unless you begin to lose track of the whole drift of thought. If you miss a few meanings sporadically, so be it: you won't remember all the footnotes anyway. Later on, review and study the material more closely. For the moment, try above all to capture the spirit of the piece.

Let's say you're reading Samuel Taylor Coleridge's "Rime of the Ancient Mariner" and come across the Mariner's vision of the dead bodies of his shipmates coming back to life:

> All stood together on the deck,
> For a charnel-dungeon fitter:
> All fixed on me their stony eyes,
> That in the Moon did glitter.

To appreciate the main point here, the speaker's horror at seeing the dead awaken, you don't need to know what a "charnel-dungeon" is. Look it up later. If you insist on doing so now, you'll lose the feel of the poem. It isn't even crucial if you don't at first understand the syntax in the second line as a whole, that the mariner is saying the dead men are fitter for a charnel-dungeon than to be walking around again on deck.

"The Rime of the Ancient Mariner" is relatively easy, as compared to other older poems. Most of its obscurities are minor enough so that you can understand and appreciate it without having to dissect it. You won't always be so fortunate. At the opposite extreme, is the refrain from the medieval lyric, "Alison," in which the speaker expresses his love-longing for the girl of the title:

> An hendy hap ic habbe yhent,
> Ichoot from hevene it is me sent:
> From alle wommen my love is lent
> And light on Alisoun.

To make any sense of this at all, you have to know the following: "hendy" means "lucky," "hap" means "chance" or "happening," "happe" means "have," "yhent" means "received," "Ichoot" means "I know," "alle" means "all the," "lent" means "taken from," and "light" means "alights" or "hit upon." But even without this knowledge, you should be able at least to respond to the remarkable music of the rhythm: the rollickingness of the "h" and "t" sounds and the short-syllables, giving way to the softer "l" sounds, and finally coming to rest on a long, drawn-out light-but-melancholy "Ali-*soooon.*"

In short, try not to let your frustrations with the linguistic difficulties of older works prevent you from appreciating what can be appreciated without toilsome study. The themes, spirit, and even techniques of older literature may be much more accessible and relevant to your concerns than you at first suspect. But don't, on the other hand, underestimate the challenge of recovering the precise meaning of a work from the remoteness of time.

2. *The Sense of Artificiality.*  Perhaps the first thing

that strikes the inexperienced reader of older literature is its *formality*. Much of it seems wordy, stuffy, pompous. Take for example the following conversation about letter-writing from *Pride and Prejudice:*

> "Oh!" cried Miss Bingley, "Charles writes in the most careless way imaginable. He leaves out half his words, and blots the rest."
>
> "My ideas flow so rapidly that I have not time to express them—by which means my letters sometimes convey no ideas at all to my correspondents."
>
> "Your humility, Mr. Bingley," said Elizabeth, "must disarm reproof."
>
> "Nothing is more deceitful," said Darcy, "than the appearance of humility. It is often only carelessness of opinion, and sometimes an indirect boast."
>
> "And which of the two do you call *my* little recent piece of modesty?"
>
> "The indirect boast;—for you are really proud of your defects in writing, because you consider them as proceeding from a rapidity of thought and carelessness of execution, which if not estimable, you think at least highly interesting."

People today don't converse like this, of course; perhaps they never did. Miss Bingley didn't literally "cry" out her speech, nor would a real-life Elizabeth be capable of such an aphorism on the spur of the moment. A contemporary Darcy might say something like, "Oh, come off it, Bingley!" and let it go at that. But Jane Austen and her contemporaries would have considered this way of proceeding much too crude. Their literary standards, like their codes of behavior, placed more emphasis on dignity, elegance, and reserve. Whereas we tend to value spontaneity and colloquialness, they valued grace and eloquence. They too believed that literary language should not deviate too far from the language of ordinary conversation, but their notion of the proper level on which to write—and converse —was basically different from ours. Ernest Hemingway's way of handling this scene, for example, would have been to duplicate the boredom of the drawing-room conversation at its most typical; Austen's approach is to show it at its most refined, to invent the kind of witty dialogue which the would-be Elizabeths and Darcys in her audience wished they could achieve in a similar situation.

One illustration naturally cannot do justice to the differences among individual writers. Some eighteenth century prose is more racy and colloquial than a good deal of the present-day fiction. But generally speaking, the experience of reading older literature for the first time is somewhat like looking through a history of costume. At first the reader is bound to wonder why people wore so many frills in the old days. Only greater familiarity can overcome this impression fully. For the present, however, it may help you to think of the difference between "polite" and colloquial levels of writing as a difference between two types of literary indirection. Compare Austen once more to Hemingway, in whose fiction the characters talk to each other in clipped phrases and the narrator's working vocabulary is mostly limited to basic English. The latter approach, as Hemingway often described it, is like the method of the iceberg: one-eighth of the meaning is stated directly and the rest is left for the reader to infer from a few simple gestures. The former approach is to talk all around, above, and below the iceberg but to make no mention of the naked object itself. Hemingway's approach is an art of elimination, restricting us to a very few clues as to what his characters are thinking; Austen's approach is an art of elaboration, providing you with all the general information you need to know about her characters but from a respectful distance.

A colloquial style has a more immediate impact on today's reader than Austen's because it is not so distracting: the reader is less likely to feel that the words are impeding what the author is trying to say. But for the experienced reader, this is actually one of the chief pleasures of such a style: it uses all the resources of which language is capable, with admirable precision and control. In Elizabeth's speech to Bingley, for instance, the tone and meaning are very complex. It is an essentially sympathetic remark by someone who nevertheless sees through Bingley's nonchalance as well as Darcy does and wants (a) to add something to the conversation, (b) to sound playful and knowing, and yet, (c) not to hurt the feelings of Bingley, whom she likes. It would probably be impossible to get this complex impression across in a paragraph of colloquial English, let alone seven words.

Perhaps the best way to build up a rapport with a more formal style is to start with prose writers where it is used wittily, as in Austen, and/or in conjunction with a strong and absorbing plot line, as in Henry Fielding's writings and certain works by Melville and Thomas Hardy.

3. *Traditionalism vs. Originality.* In addition to the points already mentioned, perhaps the most important stylistic difference between modern and older writers is their attitude toward literary tradition. Until the rise of Romanticism about 1800, innovativeness was not considered much of a literary virtue; the word originality actually had a bad connotation, like "eccentricity": the artist was advised not to strike out individually and create his own style but rather to build upon the heritage of his literary ancestors. And with a few exceptions, not until the

twentieth century did such radical stylistic innovations such as free verse, and stream-of-consciousness narration really become widespread in English and American writing.

In studying literature before 1900, therefore, it is rather important to be aware of the ways in which the works you read make use of traditional genres and conventions. The literature prior to 1900 is apt to be more influenced by these conventions than contemporary literature; also the writer presumed his audience had a knowledge of those traditions. When Shakespeare invented the so-called "dark lady" of his sonnets, for example, he did so in the realization that his audience would know that the type of lady to whom sonnets had traditionally been addressed for centuries was fair and virtuous and that his sensuous, unprincipled, dark-haired woman would be taken as a playful twist on this tradition. A few decades later, John Donne composed a sequence of "Holy Sonnets" with the awareness that his readers would find the approach daringly provocative, since sonnets had traditionally been devoted to expressing the poet's relation to a human (although idealized) beloved, not to God.

On one level, these facts simply belong in the category of literary gossip. A hard-line "new critic" might argue that the individual poems of Shakespeare and Donne should stand or fall on their own merits, to which literary tradition is really irrelevant. But this is to demand that they become something they are not, that the poems be judged in terms of our modern post-romantic cult of originality rather than in terms of the way they were written—namely, as a transformation of a previous tradition.

Since traditions are not inherited so much as ingrained over a period of time, you cannot be expected to be able to understand the ways in which a particular work draws on previous models until you have become rather well-read. And even then, you will see that the differences between the older and more recent literature are not sharply defined and complete: the two poets just mentioned did not want their work to be merely imitative, and conversely, a number of modern writers make use of traditional motifs in their work. Still, it may be useful to you for now to think of the former as a somewhat different kind of game, as far as the role of originality is concerned, a game in which the rules are stricter and more established and the objective is not to create something entirely different from what has been done before but something which will seem fresh and novel without seeming overly strange.

Most lyric poets before 1900, for example, would not have considered expressing their inspirations in a way that we today would regard as free and spontaneous, yet by skillful use of the conventions of rhythm and rhyme to which they voluntarily adhered, they managed to produce something of the same effect. Take the first stanza of Percy Shelley's poem "To a Skylark":

> Hail to thee, blithe Spirit!
> Bird thou never wert,
> That from Heaven, or near it,
> Pourest thy full heart
> In profuse strains of unpremeditated art.

A modern poet would want to handle this (as well as most any other) kind of subject and emotion in free verse. Shelley instead chooses an elaborate pattern which allows for just two rhymes, with four of the five lines very short so that every fourth or fifth word must rhyme. Today's reader may be tempted to think it is contrived, especially after seeing the same pattern repeated twenty-one times during the course of the poem. But at its best, the poem still manages to give the feeling of freedom, through the use of constant variations in the rhythm of the short lines (which is basically DA-da-DA-da-DA-da, but is altered in dozens of ways) and by the very long last line, which gives the stanza a sudden, uninhibited, swooping effect. The fact that the pattern as a whole is itself unusual and it, therefore, enhances the novelty. Altogether Shelley has carefully chosen and played by strict rules but managed to twist them to his advantage more often than not. Compared to the free expression of thought, the poem is inhibited: in its use of the patterns within which it operates, however, it is very free.

In his own way, Shelley was considered quite a rulebreaker by many of his contemporaries. So were Shakespeare, Donne, and Coleridge. This sketchy description of conventional elements in older writing has exaggerated the actual uniformity and consensus existing among writers. Throughout English literary history there have been revolutions in style and taste, corresponding to the divisions between literary eras given in the appendix. But the fact remains that for the inexperienced reader of older literature the differences between the authors just discussed seem much less dramatic than the differences between them as a group and the poetry of, say, Allen Ginsberg or Carl Sandburg.

Perhaps the best way to build up an appreciation of literature which relies strongly on traditional conventions is to avoid resting in your first reaction against their "unnaturalness," to make a practice of asking "What might the author be trying to gain from that pattern? Even though it is 'unnatural' does it increase the subtlety of the work?" Once you begin to see the subtleties, you'll forget about the unnaturalness.

### APPROACHING MODERN LITERATURE
By "modern literature" is here meant writing which is not

traditional in style, not simply all literature written during the twentieth century.* The particular type of modern literature I have in mind is that which is extremely experimental and subjective in its style, to the point that it may seem even more alien to the inexperienced reader than the literature of 400 years ago. A good deal of the fiction of Joyce and Faulkner, the poetry of T.S. Eliot and Wallace Stevens, and the plays of Samuel Beckett and Eugene Ionesco would all be good examples of this kind of writing. Historically speaking, this kind of modern literature can be seen as a logical extension of the romantic ideal of originality in literature. If originality is carried beyond a certain point, a writer's work will begin to seem unintelligible to his audience until that audience has had some special training. Fortunately, even such obscure work has its own conventions, in the sense of common traits and strategies. Here is a brief description of the principal ones.

1.  *The Problem of Fragmentariness.*  Most literature written before 1900 portrays its subjects in a way that is at least recognizable, if not exactly "realistic." You may have to struggle with the vocabulary at first but eventually you can detect a logical and/or chronological order. Modern experimental literature, however, departs from this kind of order in favor of what might be called an inner logic, in which the emphasis is on presenting the subject "as it really is" (rather than showing how it would appear to an onlooker) or as it is perceived in the mind of a particular observer (rather than trying to interpret this perspective to a third party). Here, for instance, is the way James Joyce describes what Leopold Bloom sees in a Dublin pub:

*By the same token, some literature before 1900 might be called modern. In many ways the poetry of William Blake (1757-1827), for example, is more modern than the poetry of Robert Frost (1874-1963).

> Sardines on the shelves. Almost taste them by looking. Sandwich? Ham and his descendents mustered and bred there. Potted meats. What is home without Plumtree's potted meat? Incomplete. What a stupid ad! Under the obituary notices they stuck it. All up a plumtree. Dignam's potted meat. Cannibals would with lemon and rice. White missionary too salty. Like pickled pork.

Here and elsewhere in *Ulysses,* Joyce attempts to capture the "stream of consciousness" of a very ordinary man—who proves to be quite extraordinary after all, because of the fullness with which Joyce portrays him. The fragmentary, disjointed train of thought, with its odd references, can be very difficult to follow.

Still, if you read the passage closely, with the earlier parts of the book in mind, you can understand it fairly well. It is lunchtime, so Bloom thinks of putting the sardines in a sandwich. Ham also goes in sandwiches, which leads to Bloom's very bad pun on the original Ham, the banished son of Noah in the Bible. The meat also reminds Bloom, an advertising man, of a stupid ad for Plumtree's Potted Meat; he thinks the designers of the ad were all wet—up a (plum) tree, in another bad pun. He saw the ad under the obituary notices, which recalls the funeral for Paddy Dignam which he has just attended. Poor Dignam is now reduced to potted meat, and if this were Borneo rather than Ireland, would perhaps be served up with lemon and rice.

Such are Bloom's thoughts in a split-second of time. Nor are they terribly difficult to follow, *if* (1) you have read the book attentively thus far; (2) you have a general knowledge of the Bible and (elsewhere) classical mythology: and most importantly, (3) *if you are sensitive to motif and analogy*. This is the chief way in which stream-of-consciousness narrative is organized. Instead of a logical order, the writer uses an analogical order, so to speak, defining his subject, Bloom's mind in this case, by constant repetition of its main elements in different contexts. Bloom's appetite, idle curiosity, interest in advertising, weakness for bad puns, and awareness of biblical allusions are all significant character traits which emerge repeatedly.

Looking for such patterns will help you to clear up the obscurities in a number of modern works. Another example is William Faulkner's novel, *The Sound and the Fury,* in which the first chapter consists of the reminiscences of a thirty-three-year-old idiot, Benjy Compson, presented in short snippets without regard to time sequence. But the chapter becomes much clearer as one begins to realize that Benjy continues to be preoccupied by the same basic memories and to hearken back to a few significant dates. As one reads further, his scrambled thoughts seem to fit together almost as neatly as a jigsaw puzzle.

2. *Irrationality.*   Sometimes the language and surface meaning of a modern work will be perfectly clear, but you won't have any idea whatsoever of where it all leads. Take for instance the following poem by Wallace Stevens, called "Anecdote of the Jar":

I placed a jar in Tennessee,
And round it was, upon a hill.
It made the slovenly wilderness
Surround that hill.

The wilderness rose up to it,
And sprawled around, no longer wild.
The jar was round upon the ground
And tall and of a port in air.

It took dominion everywhere.
The jar was gray and bare.
It did not give of bird or bush,
Like nothing else in Tennessee.

Here you wonder: "Why does he put a jar on the hill? Why in Tennessee, rather than in Oklahoma or Mississippi? Why a jar, for that matter? Why is the wilderness tamed?" The only solution is to continue looking until you begin to see some implications: perhaps the image is a metaphor. In this case, Stevens may be suggesting the distorting effect on nature of art, or any type of man-made construction. The jar, like any manufactured thing, tends to de-naturize the wilderness and, eventually, to dominate it. At least the person who imposes the jar on the hill is likely to see the rest of the landscape in relation to it. And the effect of this is bleak: the artist/builder has not managed to improve on nature or integrate nature into his creation: all that is left, finally, is the jar. Why a jar, rather than a bowl? Perhaps because a jar is more purely functional, less likely to be beautiful. Why Tennessee? Who knows?—perhaps not even Stevens.

Perhaps the major difference between the method of this poem and that of a pre-modern work with unusual imagery, like Donne's comparison of two lovers with a pair of compasses, is that the metaphor is left completely to implication; the reader must do the work. This of course makes the task of interpretation much more risky; it is impossible to prove that my reading of Stevens' "Anecdote" is correct. The Joyce excerpt and the Stevens' poem illustrate in this respect the general reluctance of modern writers to impose too definite a meaning on their perceptions. They view life as inherently irrational and their work reflects this quality, whether it takes the form of a mosaic of fragments like Joyce's or the more orderly presentation of an enigma, like Stevens's. To present an image or an anecdote without interpreting it is, they suggest, simply truer to the nature of things than to be explicit as to what it means, like Bryant and (to a lesser extent) Whitman.

When you feel that you have gained a certain understanding of a work which initially struck you as bizarre because it left you no clue as to what it meant, you should therefore not be too insistent on your interpretations. The Stevens poem should not be made to seem more logical than it is; the sense of disorientation which it first gave you is basic to its overall meaning. If you reduce it to a quick-and-easy parable, you will, in effect, have imposed your own jar on the wilderness of Stevens' poem.

The deadpan, matter-of-fact tone in which Stevens develops his absurd anecdote is also typical of modern writing. To take another example, Franz Kafka's short story "Metamorphosis" opens by describing in a very detached way how the main character wakes up to find that he has turned into a cockroach. We are given to understand that this is a very unfortunate turn of events, but not at all an unthinkable or impossible one. Probably the best way to understand this strangely low-keyed tone is to relate it to such modern phenomena as the city-dweller's refusal to let himself get excited by any passing event, no matter how extraordinary, or the callousness one develops as a protection against constant reports of atrocities in the mass media. To take the bizarre for granted, in other words, is for the modern writer a way of both reflecting and breaking through our own natural resistance to the constant presence of the bizarre in our daily lives.

3. *Subjectivity.* Partly because of its fondness for technical experimentation and its reluctance to draw fixed conclusions, modern literature can be fiendishly complicated, as the passage from Joyce suggests. Modern writers

frequently seem to be engaged in such games as: (a) the invention of the most intricate structures imaginable, with networks of motifs so subtle that no one can fully comprehend them; (b) the elaboration of private symbol systems or mythologies, as personal substitutes for traditional religion (D.H. Lawrence's theory of salvation by instinct and W.B. Yeats's philosophy of character based on the phases of the moon are two examples); and (c) the integration of modern thought with a range of previous religious intellectual traditions by continual use of allegory and allusion (Bloom as Ulysses is an instance of this). As a result, modern literature sometimes becomes subjective to the point that even the most sensitive and erudite critic has difficulty following the author. If you find it at first strange that W.B. Yeats describes the baby Jesus as "the uncontrollable mystery on the bestial floor" you may certainly be forgiven, because Yeats is here making use—without warning—of a theory of history held only by him.

As with reading older literature which requires a good deal of translation of one kind or another, the question becomes: is it worth finding out the information you have to know in order to understand it? Different readers take different views in each instance, of course; and when you have built up enough expertise to be able to judge for yourself, you too will have to decide whether the fact that the most ambitious modern English poem, Ezra Pound's *Cantos*, must be read with the aid of a glossary twice as long as itself should be a sufficient reason to ignore it. In the meantime, though, undoubtedly you will have become well enough initiated into some other modern writers to realize that in many cases the effort is worth making, not only because of the excellence of their work, but as a study in the workings of the artistic temperament.

There is no shortcut to this process of gradually

coming to terms with the peculiarities of a difficult modern author (or any other author), except to be aware of the three types of subjectivity just mentioned and cope with them when they arise. Each time you do, your critical instincts will improve, as will your ability to discriminate between the difficulty of a really superior artist and that of an artist who is merely confused or vague. Perhaps the best way to begin familiarizing yourself with modern literary subjectivity is to read novelists like Lawrence and Kafka, who use innovative literary techniques in the service of a personal vision but communicate that vision in a way which is more accessible to most readers than the visions of Pound or Stevens.

As you become familiar with the literature of different periods, you will come to prefer some, in general, above others. But try to avoid disparaging one at the expense of another or making premature judgments on the basis of criteria which don't really apply to what you're judging. Before allowing yourself to become disinterested in "artificiality" in older literature or by "obscurity" in contemporary writing, make an effort to understand why these qualities exist and why they are appreciated by other readers. Eventually you too may find yourself enjoying most some of the literature that baffled and alienated you upon first inspection.

# CHAPTER SIX

# WRITING ABOUT LITERATURE

The most difficult part of being a critic is the writing of criticism. Ultimately, it can be the most rewarding part also, because the process of writing forces one to refine and sharpen his thoughts; and as the methods of criticism become familiar, this process will become more a pleasure than a chore. But it is always a challenge, and at first it can be quite frustrating. "What should I write about?" and "How should I go about it?" are the two most common questions posed by students. This chapter will offer some answers.

These answers will not be completely satisfactory. First, no pre-set list of items can anticipate all the possible options which will be open to you as you sit with the work in front of you wondering what to say about it. Second, no list drawn up by another person can determine what are the best of all possible options for you. Just as every creative writer must find his own proper voice and style, so you will find with practice that certain topics and approaches work especially well for you, and you will make them your own, so to speak.

## CHOOSING A TOPIC

You will either be assigned a topic or asked to select one.

Here is a list of some topics which are commonly assigned:

1) The summary of a work (particularly for introductory-level courses)

2) Analysis of a particular character: his main traits, his development, and his role in the work as a whole

3) Discussion of an idea or problem in the work ("Is Hamlet really mad?", "What is the main theme in *Hamlet?*", etc.)

4) Discussion of the importance of the setting in a particular narrative or play

5) A close reading of the meaning and/or stylistic technique of a particular passage, perhaps also including a discussion of its importance in the work as a whole

6) Analysis of the structure of a literary work

7) The use of imagery in a work, especially poetry

8) The use of motif in a work

9) A comparison or contrast of two or more literary works

Specific hints on how to approach these topics are given not only in this book, both in preceding chapters and below, but also in the other three books in this series.

If the choice of topic is up to you, you may want to choose one of the possibilities listed above, or you may want to develop one of your own. My usual recommendation to students in search of topics is that they concentrate on something in the work which particularly struck them and try to turn it into a question. This advice doesn't work if the question is too sweeping or if its answer is already obvious, but with a little probing you should be able to find enough riddles to keep you occupied for some time.

Let's say that when reading *Hamlet* you were surprised by Hamlet's harsh treatment of Ophelia, and even more so by her sudden reaction to his snubs and her father's death: madness and suicide. You might ask yourself: "Why do they react that way?" At first, the answer to this seems obvious: Hamlet is angry that Ophelia is avoiding him at her father's request; Ophelia is distracted by the loss of both father and lover. But to let the matter drop here is only to tell you what you already know: you still haven't got past the first stage of analysis. The point of your question was really that you felt the reasons for the characters' behavior were inadequate. You felt that Hamlet ought to have been more sensitive than he was, that Ophelia should have had more stability and common sense. Now you are on the threshold of something really worth writing about. Either of these issues would be well worth pondering: (1) Why is Ophelia's character developed in a way that is psychologically improbable? Might the sudden and extreme change in her behavior have a symbolic importance in the play, even if it is apparently "unrealistic"? These questions, in turn, could lead you into a discussion of how Ophelia's development serves as both an image of and comment on Hamlet's own inner turmoil and that of the whole state as well. (2) Just how sensitive a character is Hamlet, anyway? In some respects he seems very delicate and susceptible to emotion. But in other ways he is quite callous and cruel. You might use his relationship to Ophelia as your main illustration in discussing and resolving this paradox in Hamlet's character.

Of course you might not really be interested in writing about either of these subjects at all. I mention them only as typical of the way in which one might convert a general interest in a work into an interesting piece of criticism.

As you look for possible topics to write about, here is a checklist of additional points which you may find helpful to consider.

1. *The relationship between form and content.* How does the style and method of organization contribute to

the overall meaning and effect? (Look again at the discussion of the Shakespeare sonnet and the Whitman lyric on pp. 56-58 and 64-79 for examples of this type of analysis.)

2. *Recurring elements and patterns of any kind.* Look especially for repetition and echoes in image, patterns of action, and character relationships.

3. *Alternative ways of handling a particular passage or scene or device.* Ask yourself: "Suppose the author had done Y instead of X, or suppose X had been eliminated altogether; how then would the work have been affected?"

4. *Archetypes.* Some of those most frequently used by authors include: contrasting imagery of light and darkness; religious allegory, especially Christian; the heroic quest for an ideal; the initiation into reality; and the analogy between nature and man. Be careful to pursue such issues, however, in a way which does justice to the individuality of the work: that is, to the way in which the author adapts and varies the general pattern. Nothing is less conclusive than a paper which merely proves that a given character is compared to Christ. The question should be, rather, "Just how consistent and important is this relation?"

5. *Tone.* Consider how seriously and straightforwardly the author seems to have treated whatever it is you plan to discuss. Make sure that you don't find yourself stating as an indisputable fact something at which he has only hinted, or stating as a solemn truth a point which he has treated playfully.

6. *The relevance of the various critical approaches.* Ask yourself: "What would an expressive or a mimetic approach to this work be?" In this way, interesting questions may occur to you which otherwise would have slipped by. These considerations won't always be equally helpful in the case of a given work. But in the long run it will serve you well to keep them in mind.

**PLANNING AND EXECUTING THE PAPER**

Creative writers vary greatly in their writing habits. Some can compose only in solitude: some must be out of doors. Some compose in their heads; some doodle around on the page until inspiration comes. Some use detailed outlines; some hardly seem to plan at all. Some revise extensively; others satisfy themselves (if not their audiences) the first time through. You too will and should develop those habits of composition which best suit your own personality. But here are some general suggestions.

1. *Draw up a rough outline or agenda beforehand.* A detailed outline should not be necessary for a paper of less than fifteen pages or so, unless it is required by your teacher. Indeed extensive pre-planning can inhibit you in the actual writing process, when some of your best thoughts will occur to you for the first time. But you should have a general notion of how you are going to proceed.

2. *Be sure to adjust the scope of your topic to suit the desired length of your paper.* Overcomplicated or oversimplified topics are perhaps the most frequent reasons for unsuccessful papers. As soon as you feel you might be overextending yourself, stop and review your plan for the paper as a whole. The sooner you catch yourself, the less likely you are to become trapped in an ineffective organizational framework.

3. *Do the actual writing in at least two stages.* After completing the first draft, let it sit for a while, until you have mentally detached yourself from it somewhat. The more objective and self-critical you can be when making revisions, the better will be the finished product.

**ORGANIZATION**

This will depend upon the nature of your topic. But you should be aware of the range of basic organizational models you have to choose from, and you should realize that one may be better than another in a given case. Here is a list of the main ways in which you would be likely to organize a critical paper of 2,500 words or less.

1. *The Sequential Method:* tracing your subject through a work chronologically, from beginning to end. This is the easiest method to use, because it corresponds to the way in which you read the work in the first place; and it is also the best method of handling some topics, such as the development of character. It can often hurt you, however. Let's say you chose to discuss the question of whether Hamlet is really mad, at least temporarily, instead of just pretending. In developing this topic, the easiest method would be to write your paper in the form of a running commentary of Hamlet's behavior from Act I through Act V of the play. To do this, however, would almost inevitably lead you into a great deal of unnecessary summarizing. You would find yourself writing in this vein:

> *We first see Hamlet in the courtroom scene in Act I.* Here he speaks strangely to the king and queen, *who seem to be trying to make peace with him;* but he seems to be alienated or distracted rather than really mad. This impression is strengthened during his first soliloquy, *which tells us why he is so bitter toward his mother and uncle. Later on, he meets the ghost on the battlements.* This experience clearly has an unsettling effect on his mind.

This passage contains a good deal of information which is peripheral, if not altogether irrelevant, to your topic. The italicized parts are almost entirely excess baggage—yet you will find them and phrases like them very hard to resist if you follow the running commentary approach; otherwise your paper will become a hopelessly disjointed collection

of fragmentary insights. In fact it may become that anyway. To continue the method of this passage throughout a
four-page paper would create the same impression as looking at a painting with a microscope from left to right. A
much better way in which to organize your topic in this
case would be:

2. *The Analytical Method.* dividing your subject into
aspects or arguments and developing them point by point.
For example, formulate several considerations which argue
for and against the idea that Hamlet is really mad, then
discuss each in turn, introducing evidence from the various
scenes in the play as it seems appropriate. This approach
will require a good deal more forethought, but it will also
produce much more satisfying results. Not every topic
should be developed in this way, but it usually is the best
method for organizing a discussion of any argument, abstract idea, or general issue as applied to the work. Even a
paper on the development of Hamlet's character would
benefit from a section of general remarks about his primary
characteristics, in addition to discussing his behavior from
scene to scene.

3. *The Comparative Method:* discussions of different works, characters, themes, critical theories, and the like
usually are organized in one or two ways, corresponding to
the two methods just described. The first might be called
the "A then B" method, in which each item to be compared is discussed in turn. The second is the analytical or
point-by-point method, in which points of comparison are
isolated and the various items compared under each head.
Except in very short papers, the second method is almost
always preferable, for it enables one to focus and refine
his comparisons much better than the first. Unless one is
very careful, the "A then B" method leads to the same
sort of digressiveness as in the *Hamlet* example, and the

result is two or three mini-papers instead of one coherent essay. Let's say, for example, that you were planning to compare Shakespeare's plays with his poetry, using *Hamlet* and the sonnet discussed earlier as your main illustrations. You *could* handle this topic by examining each work in succession for features which seem to recall each other. Your paper would be much more organized and focused, however, if you arranged it in terms of comparable features, such as: preoccupation with the themes of mortality and male companionship, fondness for metaphorical language, and the innovative use of traditional literary forms.

Even then your organization might leave something to be desired, if the various points of comparison were as unrelated to each other as in the example just given. In this case, it would be well to limit your scope further by concentrating solely on the use of common themes in the two types of works. As you develop a comparative paper, finally, do not hesitate to acknowledge differences as well as similarities. Do not let yourself be trapped into implying that Shakespeare's plays and sonnets are exactly alike.

4. *The Microcosm Method:* using one or two central passages around which to build your discussion of a work or author. As a rule, you should begin with the quotation, explain its meaning and style to the extent that seems necessary, and then single out a given number of ways in which you feel it typifies or illustrates your subject as a whole. For instance, you might use a close examination of one of Hamlet's longer speeches as the basis for a paper analyzing his character. Sometimes you may be required to use this format, as an exercise in the art of close reading; in some other cases as well, you may find it a useful way of organizing your thoughts about a work. If you pick your key passage well, you will very likely be able to trace the

main qualities of the work through it. The risks are, first, that the passage will be an incomplete or insufficiently representative illustration of your subject, and second, that you may find yourself straining too hard to read ingenious meanings into the passage. (Perhaps you may have had that reaction to my use of the method in Chapter Four.) Altogether, the microcosm approach should be used sparingly, although in some cases it is very helpful.

5. *The "Poetic" Method:* giving your reactions to the work in an impressionistic rather than reasoned form. This is the riskiest of all the methods, often leading to a dreamy mishmash of verbiage which may mean a great deal to the writer but nothing to anybody else. But if you have a gift for language, the method may be worth trying at those times when you have very strong impressions about a work which you don't think can be adequately expressed in a regular analysis. Ordinarily, the solution in such a case is to let the work settle a bit in your mind before you write about it. Still, a creative thinker can sometimes discover and convey valuable insights about a work by letting his mind roam more freely than a logical framework will permit. Since creativity in criticism depends a good deal on training and discipline, however, you should probably resist the temptation to write poetic analyses until you have had a fair amount of experience in reading and studying literature.

This short survey of organizational models does not cover all the possibilities by any means, but it should at least be enough to get you started.

### GENERAL SUGGESTIONS ABOUT STYLE

1. *Don't belabor the obvious.* Be concise. Explain and illustrate your points fully enough to make yourself understood but don't include unnecessary information.

Don't begin by writing "the purpose of this paper is to discuss the theme of madness in one of the most famous plays by William Shakespeare (1564-1616), the tragedy of *Hamlet*" when it would be sufficient to say "The purpose of this paper is to discuss the theme of madness in Shakespeare's *Hamlet.*" Most of the critical papers you will be asked to write will be quite short, so that habitual wordiness will hurt you badly. Remember also that in most cases the audience for whom you're writing (usually the teacher) will already be familiar with the work you're discussing. Unless your teacher directs you otherwise, you should assume a certain sophistication in your reader and not write as if your paper were intended for an audience which knew nothing about literature.

2. *Don't summarize. Analyze.* Simply to summarize the story or argument of a work is not to say anything very meaningful about it, especially if the work has been discussed in class. To be sure, it takes a good deal of concentration and exactness to write a good summary, and for this reason your teacher may sometimes require such an assignment of you—as part of a book report, for instance. But as a rule you should avoid summarizing during an analysis except when you believe your reader really needs to be informed of what happens in the work, for a summary deals only with the surface of a work and says nothing more about it than a moderately attentive person can gather from one quick reading. Many students seem to feel compelled always to summarize whatever they intend to discuss, and the result. is usually that they leave themselves very little time to discuss it. Their finished papers, therefore, show little evidence that they have thought about their subject in any depth.

3. *Don't be too argumentative.* As a critic, your purpose is to tell the truth about your subject, rather than

to argue your case like a lawyer; and the best way to do
this in most instances is not to be too one-sided but to
look at your topic in the round. As we have seen, literature
is often ambiguous, paradoxical, and indefinite in its
implications and patterns, and this leads to conflicting interpretations. Your job should not be to perpetuate these con-
flicts by fighting down the line for one side or another but
to consider and evaluate the various alternatives. You will
be truer to your subject if you approach literature in the
spirit of "on the one hand. . .on the other hand," than as if
you approach it in the spirit of a polemic. Do not hesitate, however, to speak strongly if you really have strong
convictions about a work. Nor should you hesitate on
occasion to oversimplify some points in order to present
a position which you consider especially important, as
long as you indicate that you know what you are doing. In
general, however, the best literary criticism takes account
of possible exceptions and objections to its claims even as
it states them. A paper full of assertions like "This
is the greatest twentieth-century novel" or "So-and-so is an
incredibly complicated character" will sound gushy and un-
convincing even if it happens to be talking about *Ulysses*
and Leopold Bloom. A paper on Bloom which considered
only his resemblances to the original Ulysses without con-
sidering the differences (or vice-versa) would sound equally
indiscriminate.

    4. *Quotations can be useful, but don't get carried
away by them.* Use quotations (a) to illustrate special
qualities in a work which can't be conveyed in plain prose;
(b) to serve as a basis for analysis; and (c) if they are
striking, to underline a point you want to make. But avoid
(a) repeated illustrations of the same point; (b) excessively
long quotations (a good rule of thumb is: don't take any
more space on a long quotation than the amount of space

you are prepared to spend in analyzing it); and (c) continual quotation-dropping for the sake of effect. Several well-chosen quotations can enhance your writing greatly, but nothing is more annoying than a paper which amounts to little more than a patchwork of snippets. The actual amount you should quote from paper to paper will of course depend upon the nature of your topic, the nature of the work, and the specific requirements of your instructor.

5. *Avoid excessive subjectiveness.* Some student papers can be reduced to one basic sentence: "this book is good (bad) because I do (don't) like it." To be sure, any piece of literary analysis, even by professional critics, will reflect the personal preferences of the writer. But the difference between good and bad criticism in this respect is the ability to explain one's preferences so as to make them seem plausible and—ideally—convincing and illuminating to a second person. The reader of professional criticism is interested in learning what the critic has to say about the work, not in the critic's private feelings. The same applies to student papers. However strong your personal reaction to a work happens to have been, it will not impress your reader unless it enables you to write perceptively about the work itself.

6. *But don't distrust your own responses.* In the first and last analysis, they are what you have to go on. Try to hang onto your original reactions to the work, and don't let them get lost in the effort of writing the way you feel you are supposed to. Even if you have trouble getting good results from papers on literature, the chances are that your reactions to what you read are not wrong, but that you simply need to examine them more closely, to express them more fully and precisely. If you come up with what seems to be an eccentric notion about a work you read, don't get carried away by it, but don't repudiate it either.

Play around with it in your mind, and see what you can make of it. Don't forget about it just because it doesn't seem to fit conveniently into a particular hypothesis. It may turn out to be a contribution to the understanding of the work which nobody else could have made.

Perhaps the best way to sum up this discussion of critical writing is to say that the best critical paper you can write is the one which most nearly manages to capture and convey the strength, depth, and complexity of your reaction to the work or subject it discusses. Undoubtedly, the best you can do is not as good as you will be able to do some day. But that should not discourage you. On the contrary, one of the best things about criticism is that the critic is continually surprising himself with new discoveries, not only about literature but about himself as well.

*APPENDIX*

## THE MAJOR PERIODS OF ENGLISH AND AMERICAN LITERARY HISTORY

### I. ENGLISH LITERATURE*

| Name of period; subdivisions if any | dates | | some important authors, works |
|---|---|---|---|
| **Medieval Period** | ca. | 450-ca. 1500 | |
| Anglo-Saxon or Old English Period | ca. | 450-ca. 1100 | *Beowulf* |
| Anglo-Norman Period | ca. | 1100-ca. 1350 | (French the language of educated classes) |
| Middle English Period | ca. | 1350-ca. 1500 | Geoffrey Chaucer |
| | | | The Pearl Poet |
| | | | Thomas Malory |
| **Renaissance Period** | ca. | 1500-ca. 1560 | John Skelton |
| Early Tudor Period | ca. | 1500-ca. 1560 | Edmund Spencer |
| Elizabethan Period | ca. | 1560- 1603 | Sir Philip Sidney |
| | | | Christopher Marlowe |
| | | | William Shakespeare |
| | | | Ben Jonson |

*Most of the names and divisions refer to monarchs and the dates of their reigns rather than literary events. The only outstanding exception is the dating of the Romantic period from 1798, when William Wordsworth and Samuel T. Coleridge published their *Lyrical Ballads*. As the repetitions of some names in the right-hand column suggest, not all authors can be easily pigeonholed.

|  |  |  |
|---|---|---|
| Jacobean Period | 1603- 1625 | William Shakespeare<br>Ben Jonson<br>Sir Francis Bacon |
| Caroline Period | 1625- 1649 | John Donne<br>John Donne<br>Robert Herrick<br>John Milton<br>John Milton |
| Commonwealth Period | 1649- 1660 | |
| Neoclassical Period | 1660- 1798 | |
| Restoration Period | 1660- 1700 | William Congreve<br>John Dryden |
| Eighteenth Century | 1700- 1798 | |
| Augustan Age | 1700-ca. 1750 | Alexander Pope<br>Jonathan Swift<br>Henry Fielding<br>Samuel Richardson |
| Later Eighteenth Century<br>(also called Pre-Romantic Period;<br>Age of Johnson) | ca. 1750- 1798 | Samuel Johnson<br>Richard B. Sheridan<br>Laurence Sterne |
| Romantic Period | 1798-ca. 1830 | William Wordsworth<br>Samuel T. Coleridge<br>George Gordon, Lord Byron<br>Percy Shelley<br>John Keats<br>Sir Walter Scott |

| Name of period; subdivisions if any | dates | some important authors, works |
| --- | --- | --- |
| **Victorian Period**.............. | ca. 1830-   1901 | Alfred Lord Tennyson<br>Robert Browning<br>Matthew Arnold<br>Charles Dickens<br>William Thackeray<br>George Eliot<br>Thomas Hardy<br>Oscar Wilde |
| **Edwardian Period** ......... | 1901-ca. 1914 | Arnold Bennett<br>Joseph Conrad<br>George Bernard Shaw |
| **Modern Period** ......... | ca. 1914-ca. 1945 | Joseph Conrad<br>George Bernard Shaw<br>D.H. Lawrence<br>W.B. Yeats<br>James Joyce<br>Virginia Woolf<br>T.S. Eliot<br>W.H. Auden<br>Dylan Thomas |
| **Contemporary Period**........... | ca. 1945-present | W.H. Auden<br>Anthony Powell<br>Anthony Burgess<br>Harold Pinter<br>Ted Hughes |

## II. AMERICAN LITERATURE

| | | | |
|---|---|---|---|
| Colonial Period ............... | 1607- | 1776 | Edward Taylor<br>Benjamin Franklin<br>Jonathan Edwards |
| Early National Period......... | 1776-ca. 1830 | | Philip Freneau<br>Charles B. Brown |
| Romantic Period.............. | ca. 1830-ca. 1865 | | R.W. Emerson<br>Henry Thoreau<br>Nathaniel Hawthorne<br>Herman Melville<br>Emily Dickinson<br>Walt Whitman<br>Edgar Allan Poe |
| Realistic Period............... | ca. 1865-ca. 1914 | | |
| Age of Realism............... | ca. 1865-ca. 1900 | | Mark Twain<br>William Howells<br>Henry James |
| Age of Naturalism ........... | ca. 1900-ca. 1940* | | Theodore Dreiser<br>John Dos Passos<br>John Steinbeck<br>Richard Wright |

*Naturalism occurs in two waves, corresponding roughly to the first and third decades of the century.

| Name of period; subdivisions if any | dates | some important authors, works |
|---|---|---|
| **Modern Period** .................. | ca. 1915-ca. 1945 | Ernest Hemingway<br>F. Scott Fitzgerald<br>Ezra Pound<br>Wallace Stevens<br>William Faulkner<br>William Carlos Williams |
| **Contemporary Period**.............. | ca. 1945-present | Saul Bellow<br>Flannery O'Connor<br>Theodore Roethke<br>John Barth |

# FOR FURTHER READING

I. **Information about the Various Critical Approaches**

Abrams, M.H. *The Mirror and the Lamp: Romantic Theory and the Critical Tradition.* New York: Oxford Univ. Press, 1953; Norton paperback reprint, 1958. Pp. 3-29.

—A difficult but valuable overview of the four major approaches discussed in Chapter Two.

Adams, Hazard. *The Interests of Criticism: An Introduction to Literary Theory.* New York: Harcourt paperback, 1969.

—A survey of the main critical theories; organized historically; designed for college students.

Gross, Laila, ed. *An Introduction to Literary Criticism.* New York: Capricorn paperback, 1972.

—Contains selections from thirteen eminent critics from Aristotle to the present, representing all major critical approaches. Often very difficult reading, but a good place to go if you want to sample what the great critics have said about the methods of criticism.

Guerin, Wilfred, and Earle Labor, Lee Morgan, and John Willingham. *A Handbook of Critical Approaches to Literature.* New York: Harper paperback, 1966.

—The next step up from Chapters Two and Four of this book, in the level of difficulty. Discusses various critical approaches, distinguishing many more than the basic ones outlined here, applying them to particular works in detail. Often superficial and inaccurate, but of some use nonetheless.

Scott, Wilbur. *Five Approaches to Literary Criticism: An Arrangement of Contemporary Critical Essays.* New York: Macmillan paperback, 1962.

—Explanations of the major critical approaches (using a somewhat different organizational scheme than is followed in this book), together with examples of each. Less abstract than Abrams, more sophisticated than Guerin et al.

## II.    Histories of Literature

Daiches, David. *A Critical History of English Literature.* 2 vols. New York: Ronald, 1960.

—A readable, survey-appreciation of the high points of English literature from start to finish. Unfortunately, there is no really comparable work for American literature. The closest approximation is

Spiller, Robert, and Willard Thorp, Thomas Johnson, Henry Canby, and Richard Ludwig, editors. *Literary History of the United States.* 2 vols., 3rd edition. New York: Macmillan, 1963.

—A collection of essays by various critics about major writers and trends from the beginning of American literature to the present.

## III.    Reference Works

Abrams, M.H. *A Glossary of Literary Terms.* New York: Holt paperback, 1957.

—Definitions of most commonly-used terms. See also the glossaries in the other books in this series.

Hart, James D. *The Oxford Companion to American Literature* 4th edition. New York and London: Oxford Univ. Press, 1965.

—A short encyclopedia of authors, trends, and events.

Harvey, Paul. *The Oxford Companion to English Literature.* 4th edition, revised by Dorothy Eagle, Oxford: Clarendon Press, 1967.

—Same format as the preceding volume.

*The Oxford Dictionary.* 12 vols. and supplement. Oxford: Clarendon Press, 1933.

—Supplies definitions of words for all periods of English literary history beginning with the Middle Ages.